A
Quick
History
of

IDAHO SPRINGS

By Beth Simmons

WESTERN REFLECTIONS
PUBLISHING COMPANY®
Lake City, Colorado

Dedicated to

Alvin and Patricia Mosch
Mountain Mentors to the Masses

ISBN 978-1-932738-08-7

Library of Congress Control Number: 2004110305

Cover illustration: Charlie Tayler Water Wheel and Bridal Veil Falls by
Caroline Jensen
Cover and text design by Laurie Goralka Design

Printed in the United States of America

Western Reflections Publishing Company®
P.O. Box 1149
951 N. Highway 149
Lake City, CO 81235
www.westernreflectionspublishing.com

Table Of Contents

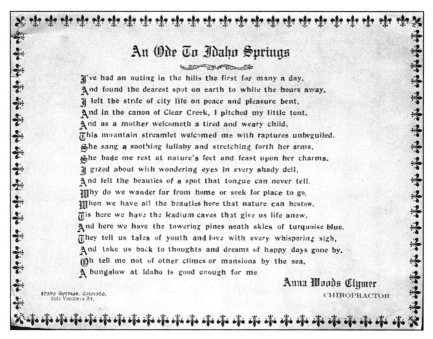

Ode to Idaho Springs by Dr. Anna Woods Clymer (Courtesy Historical Society of Idaho Springs)

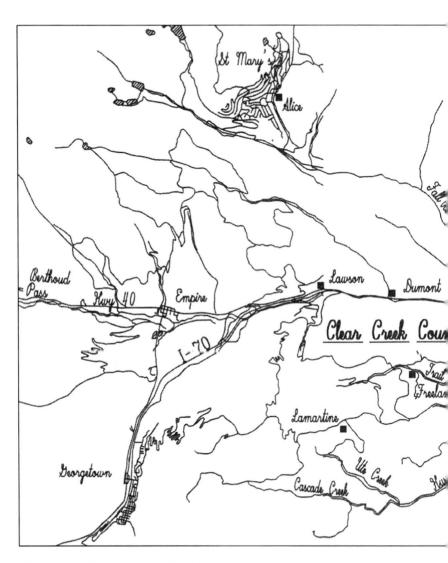

Clear Creek County by Greg Markel

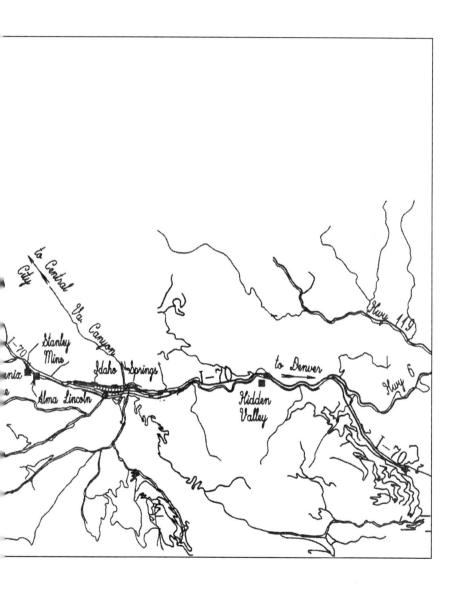

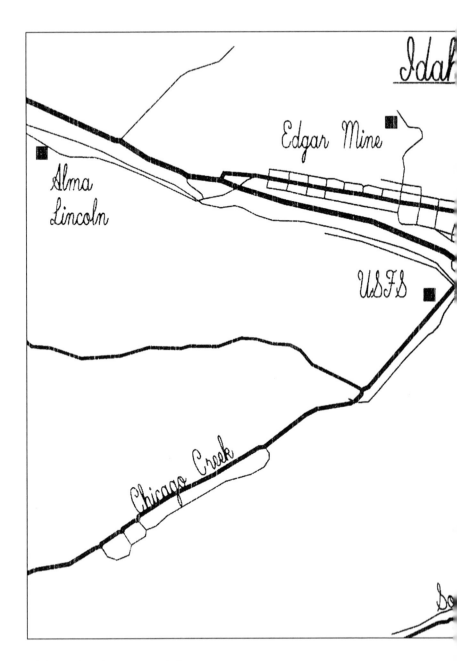

Idaho Springs by Greg Markel

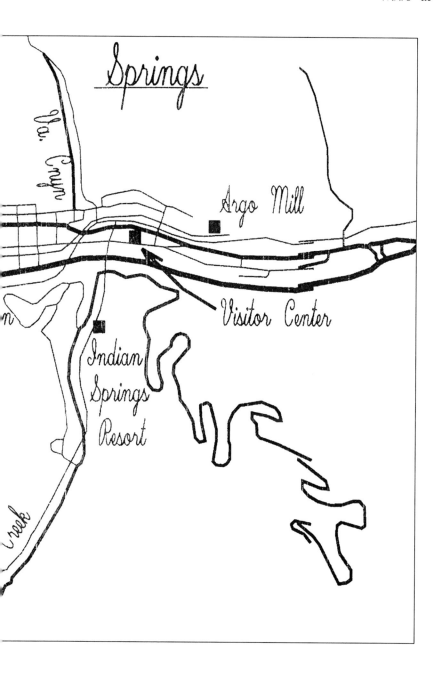

Driving seventy miles per hour along Interstate 70 through Clear Creek Valley and Idaho Springs hardly prepares the casual tourist for the treasure trove between the mountains that rise up on either side of the road. One must get off the beaten path to explore the spectacular canyons and historic mining town that has beckoned to gold and health seekers for a century and a half.

It was here, on January 7, 1859, just before a snowstorm, that George Andrew Jackson, cousin of Kit Carson, tried his luck at panning and filled his tin cup with a gold nugget and gold dust. From that find began the "Pikes Peak Gold Rush," the biggest gold rush and immigration in American history. Since then, the mountains of this section of the Front Range have produced millions upon millions of dollars in gold, silver, copper, lead, zinc, uranium, tellurium, and molybdenum.

West of Idaho Springs were the Lamartine, Alma-Lincoln and the Freeland Mines, as well as the Whale and the Hukill that later became part of the Stanley Mine. The Champion and the Specie Payment Mines sat high on the southern slope of Bellevue Mountain. On Seaton Mountain were the Treasure Vault, the Two Brothers, the Metropolitan, Fourth of July, Dove's Nest, Franklin, and Gem Mines. The Edgar, north of Idaho Springs, and Dixie Mine, in Ute Creek, were great producers. Along Fall River, the mines of Alice and Yankee Hill filled the financial coffers of the astute businessmen who invested in, mined, and managed these valuable resources.

Modern Idaho Springs, 2002, Don Allan Photo (Courtesy Historical Society of Idaho Springs)

Early Idaho Springs, 1887 (Courtesy Historical Society of Idaho Springs)

Huge gold-processing mills once lined the banks of Clear Creek. In Idaho Springs alone over two dozen mills and sampling works treated ore from the area's mines. Today, the Argo Mill and the buildings of the Stanley Mine testify to the region's dependence on the wealth within the earth. Other mills lined the banks of the mountains alongside Clear Creek all the way to Silver Plume. The ingenious mill designers used the topography to help the ore roll downhill in the mill operations.

Before front-end loaders, trucks, conveyers, and collapsed surface-mining techniques came into vogue, entrepreneurs bored great tunnels into the mountains to access the veins from below. Around Idaho Springs, at least a dozen large tunnel projects pulled ore from the mines. The Argo Tunnel was the longest, but many others like the Big Five, the Rockford, the Metropolitan, the Merrimac, the Freeland, the Lamartine, the McClelland, the Lucania, and the Burns-Moore intersected hundreds of veins. They provided transportation and drainage for the labyrinth of drifts and stopes in the mountains above and below the tunnel level.

During the late 1800s and early 1900s, Idaho Springs was a center of technological advancement in mining engineering and techniques. Nicknamed the "Buckle of the Mineral Belt," many "new-fangled" devices such as electricity, pneumatic drills, flotation, and the Edison Process found their way into the industry early in Clear Creek County.

The nearby mountains have produced all sorts of minerals. Mica was mined for insulators during World War II; "steel galena" that came from Clear Creek County mines enabled crystal radios to receive signals during the 1920s and during the 1950s, uranium ore came from many old gold mines. Now, the Henderson Mine operation in Clear Creek County boasts that it is the nation's leader in molybdenum production. The old Edgar Mine, operated by the Colorado School of Mines, is active as a testing site for modern mining techniques and equipment companies.

The town's name comes from the famed hot springs that James Jack and son first discovered in 1860 while sinking a shaft through the gravel of Soda Creek bed to solid rock beneath. Reaching a depth of eighteen inches, hot water gushed into their hole.[1] Today, the hot springs still issue forth, their waters now flowing into the hot tubs and swimming pools of the Indian Springs Resort. Even though mining dominated the development of the region, with its hot springs and nearby alpine scenery, Idaho Springs quickly grew into a tourist destination.

The numerous canyons that feed waters into Clear Creek once held glaciers that have long since melted. South of the town, from the top of Mount Evans accessed by the highest paved road in the world, tourists view a 360° panorama. The great mountain swale called South Park lies far to the southwest. The hump of Pikes Peak, which gave its name to the gold rush, juts above the hills of Cripple Creek, "the world's greatest mining camp," about eighty miles south. To the north, Rocky Mountain National Park's landmark sentinel, Longs Peak, dominates the skyline. To the east, the vast ocean of prairie extends as far as the eye can see.

Come explore the treasures of eastern Clear Creek County, Colorado.

CHAPTER ONE

George Jackson's Camp

George Andrew Jackson was twenty-four years old when he came through Colorado in the summer of 1858.[2] His cousin, the famous Kit Carson, had taken the young lad to California with him in 1852 and had taught Jackson to hunt, trap, and pan for gold. Literature tells us that Jackson came as far west as the Forks of Clear Creek during August of 1858,[3] while other early day prospectors were panning in Cherry Creek, the South Platte River, and Ralston Creek. At that time, Clear Creek was called "Vasquez Fork of the South Platte" after Louis Vasquez, the great fur trader and mountain man, who probably hunted and trapped in the valley and who may have established a temporary trading post at its mouth in the 1830s.[4]

During the fall of 1858, a mining camp called Arapahoe Bar was established along Clear Creek near the mouth of Ralston Creek. Louis Ralston and John Beck had panned some of the first gold at that site in Vasquez Fork eight years earlier on June 20, 1850.[5]

In the Idaho Springs area, lode gold comes from ancient fault zones that carried fluids rich with metals during more recent volcanic episodes. Metals, including gold, filled the cracks and crevices. As the mountains were uplifted, the veins were exposed at the surface. Gold withstands the chemical changes of weathering longer than iron or copper, and eventually water erodes the vein and carries miniscule gold flecks into a stream. There, bacteria that live in acid water ingest the gold, "fix it," and add to the mass, creating gold nuggets. Deposits of gold or other precious minerals such as sapphires or diamonds in gravels are called "placers." One of the largest gold nuggets ever found in Colorado weighed one pound. Joel Parker Whitney purchased it from the miner in California Gulch across the Divide in 1865 for $300.[6]

The Arapahoe Indians often camped at the mouth of Ralston Creek over the winter, and it was frequently referred to as "Arapahoe City." Working out of the camp with his partners, Thomas Golden and James Saunders, Jackson prospected along the Front Range. Saunders (sometimes spelled Sanders) may have been a half-breed who went by the name "Black Hawk."

After Christmas Day of 1858, the three men took a cart and yoke of oxen up an old Ute trail into the hills on a trip hunting for meat for the camp. They arrived at "Elk Park," about seven miles southwest of the main camp on Clear Creek where they stopped at a spring in an aspen grove. From there, Jackson went a mile or so west and killed five elk cows and one bull. Saunders shot a deer and two elk, and Golden killed two deer. The next day, Jackson followed an elk trail west to the brow of the mountain where he could look down on Vasquez Fork. Coming upon a herd of 600 elk, he killed a fat cow, then he made camp on top of the ridge. The next day — the last day of the year — after leaving Golden and Saunders with the dressed-out kill to return to the main camp, he plowed his way through the snow down the side of the valley to the creek. By dark he had made camp beside the stream.[7]

The next day, January 1, 1859, Jackson, traveling with his two dogs, went upstream about eight miles and camped at the site of the future mineral springs. He killed "a fat sheep" from a flock of about a thousand that were grazing in the grassy valley.[8]

On the second day of the year, his growling dogs awakened Jackson just in time to see a mountain lion dragging off his freshly killed sheep. He shot at the lion, hitting him in the shoulder, then followed the beast out of camp and finished him off. On January 3, Jackson hiked up Vasquez Fork to "where a tributary came in from the south."[9] The next day, he explored farther upstream and found his way up what is now called Fall River.[10] In the previous fall, October 1858, William Green Russell, founder of Auraria and one of the leaders of the gold rush, had explored the upper reaches of this great gold-laden valley.[11]

When Jackson returned to camp, he discovered that another mountain lion had eaten his meat. The next day, he moved his camp up to the gravel bars at the mouth of the stream coming into Vasquez Fork from the south, the one that he had described the day before, now called Chicago Creek. He panned a few cups of gravel with no success. The next day, a wolverine came into camp and the dogs were hurt wrestling with the creature. With Jackson's help, they killed it.[12]

On the seventh day, Jackson hit pay dirt. His diary records:

> *Removed fire embers and dug into rim on bed rock — Panned out eight treaty cups of dirt and [found] nothing but fine colors — 9th cup I got one nugget coarse gold — feel good tonight.*[13]

How far is it to the Jackson Monument? A promotional ploy to direct all travelers to Idaho Springs, 1930s (Courtesy Historical Society of Idaho Springs)

George Andrew Jackson (Courtesy Colorado Historical Society #F-2530-10033115)

A huge stone monument placed in 1909 marks the site of Jackson's Bar in the Clear Creek County Middle School parking lot.

Between fighting a snowstorm and taking time to nurse his injured dogs, Jackson took a week to return to Arapahoe City. When he got there, Saunders was gone and Jackson shared the news of his nugget find with Golden. They vowed to keep it secret until they could find the money to return and explore and mine it properly.[14]

In the meantime, men from Nebraska were mining placer gold at Gold Hill in what is now Boulder County. On January 17, 1859, they established the first permanent mining camp at Gold Hill.[15] On April 23, 1859, William Byers announced in the first issue of the *Rocky Mountain News* that E.L. Goodwin had found gold in a quartz vein in Gold Hill.[16] That was the first lode vein found by Americans in what is now Colorado.

Another argonaut named John Gregory, prevented from going to the Alaskan gold fields by winter weather, came south along the Front Range from Fort Laramie. He prospected up and down the canyons along the mountains and apparently talked to Jackson about the location of the discovery at Vasquez Fork.[17]

By April, Jackson found a group of men from Chicago willing to grub-stake his claim. On April 17, 1859, the Jackson group, now equipped for mining, headed west up Clear Creek toward Jackson's discovery. The group managed to hack their way through the thick underbrush along the creek banks. They repeatedly had to take their wagons apart to get through and across the creek. It took the trailblazers two weeks to make the trip to the gold-rich bars of Clear Creek.[18] The same trek requires today's traveler about thirty minutes.

Once the "Chicago Company" arrived in the valley around the hot springs, they began mining in earnest on May 6, 1859.[19] They officially established a mining camp, complete with mining laws, on May 9, 1859.[20]

About the same time, Gregory was exploring and prospecting North Clear Creek, the branch of Clear Creek that flows through the present-day town of Black Hawk. On May 6, 1859, he discovered the great vein that bears his name, the Gregory Lode. Historians cite this date as the official beginning of the Colorado mining industry.

William Byers, the hotshot young publisher of the *Rocky Mountain News*, was at the scene at Jackson's Bar. When he heard of Gregory's find, he rushed up Virginia Canyon to what became Gregory Gulch to get the scoop. The trip took him two days.

The camp at Jackson's Bar grew quickly; over 200 gold seekers came into the valley in less than a month. One member of Jackson's party, James Payne, claimed the land on the north side of the creek. He entertained miners at "Payne's Bar" nightly with his violin playing.

On May 10, 1859, the day after that first town meeting, Andrew Sagendorf and Ransom P. Smith discovered the Spanish Bar, a mile-long, rich gravel bar west of Idaho Springs.[21] The Americans called the

The Spanish Bar, c. 1865, Charles Weitfle photo (Courtesy Denver Public Library Western History Collection #X-21788)

deposit the "Spanish Bar" because of old stone gold mills or "arrastras," that they claimed to have found in the streambed and that they assumed had been built by early Spanish prospectors.

Who had been here earlier? There is a large square hole high above the Spanish Bar in the barren rocks on the south side of Clear Creek. For lack of a better explanation, locals believe that the hole was a Spanish look-out site, because from that high spot a person can see to the end of the valley. Another postulation is that the hole may have been a sign marking the site of the rich gold below. The dump from the excavation is completely overgrown.[22] Had the Mexican miners who came with John Simpson Smith and dug at the Dry Creek Diggings south of Denver in 1857 found their way up Clear Creek? Or were these much earlier diggings? Records do not reveal the origin of the early diggings or of the look-out hole, but when the early gold miners arrived they reportedly found the remains of a large, log house at the confluence of the West Branch of Clear Creek and the main trunk of Clear Creek at the base of Douglas Mountain. Had Vasquez and his men come this way in the 1830s and tried their hand at mining?

Within the month, Jackson sold his claim on Jackson's Bar to the Chicago Company for a "goodly sum" and headed toward new finds in South Park. By the end of the year, every streambed around Idaho Springs was lined with arrastras, long toms, rocker boxes, sluice boxes, prospect buckets, winches, mine dumps, and tents.

Many placer deposits in the Idaho Springs area were worked out of drifts, shafts, and tunnels that were constructed in the gravel. Timbering the tunnels was a tremendous job, because the gravels caved in easily. Many early miners were killed by cave-ins of the tunnels that now underlie Idaho Springs.

In the two years after American settlement, the Spanish Bar produced $2 million in gold nuggets. In today's world, that gold would be worth about $35 million.

The permanent settlement of the valley began, as shopkeepers and bakers, blacksmiths, and doctors came to practice their trade, panning a little gold in their spare time. One of those bakers was Augusta Tabor, with her baby in her arms, devotedly followed her husband, Horace, west in his quest for gold.[23]

A man whose future daughter-in-law was to play a large part in the Tabors' future was William Doe who came from Oshkosh, Wisconsin, to Central City in the early 1860s. He preached the first sermon there and claimed the Fourth of July Mine on Seaton Mountain, just north of Idaho Springs.

In 1877, well after Horace and Augusta Tabor were established in Leadville, William Doe sent for his son, Harvey, and Harvey's beautiful blonde young wife, the former Elizabeth Bonduel McCourt.[24] They came to Central City to manage the Fourth of July Mine for Harvey's father. Harvey, bowing to the pressures of supporting a wife, proved to be a drunk. "Baby" Doe had an affair with the local clothing store owner, and in 1879, after her baby was stillborn, Elizabeth divorced Harvey in Denver.[25]

"Baby" Doe, with her lover's pleading, then went to Leadville, where, in 1880, William Bush, who knew her in Central City, introduced her to Horace Tabor.[26] The Central City Opera annually immortalizes the rest of the story, the legend of their romance, in the "Ballad of Baby Doe."

After a trip back to Wisconsin to tend to his lumber business, William Doe returned first to Central City to tend to his son's doings, then to Idaho Springs. Doe then discovered some paying claims on Columbia Mountain near Empire. Doe bought the Bank of Idaho Springs from Charles R. Fish in 1881 and was elected Clear Creek County legislator where he served as speaker of the House. In 1883, the bank was reorganized into the First National Bank. William Doe died in 1884 while his former daughter-in-law's escapades with Horace Tabor made the society pages near and far.[27] Harvey Doe remarried in 1893 and worked as a cigar-maker in Oshkosh, Wisconsin, then as a hotel detective in Milwaukee, where he died in 1921.[28]

CHAPTER TWO

The Earliest Days in Idaho Springs

It wasn't long before the vast wealth of the region's rocks became widely known. Prospectors probed every stream and mountainside in search of metallic riches. Crude cabins sprang up along the valleys. John Hukill discovered the first vein just west of Idaho Springs on the north side of the creek. Then came the discovery of the Whale Lode on the south side. Later, miners discovered that these veins were the same. The prospectors found other veins that crossed Clear Creek and that cropped out in the many gulches that radiated down out of the mountains into the valley.

At first the veins were easy to work. Mother Nature had weathered those gold veins until nothing remained but free gold and iron-rich "gossan," the name Cornish miners applied to weathered ore at the surface. The miners ground the mineral-rich rock in arrastras, then panned out the free gold that awaited them.

Then they hit the "cap rock" or unweathered sulfide-rich ore. By 1863, the weathered zones of the major veins had been worked out and the easy pickings were gone. Technology had yet to produce a method to recover gold from the deeper ore. So, miners abandoned their cabins and claims for the new placer fields of Leadville, Breckenridge, and along the Swan and Blue Rivers.

Because of water shortages, cave-ins, and slow going in the placer deposits at Idaho Springs, other miners moved to more profitable lode deposits in Black Hawk and Empire. At that time, numerous deserted cabins greeted William Byers on his trek up Clear Creek. He reported in his *Rocky Mountain News* that:

> *Too many crowded in, in early days, built houses and mills, and laid out towns, before they knew whether they could find paying mines or not. The result of subsequent operations, when it come to piercing the cap, or hoisting the huge boulders out of bar claims, did not fill their expectations and in utter disgust they left for other diggings.*[29]

However, some kept the faith. *The News* continued:

> *Notwithstanding the apparent dullness, miners along the creek have never had a better season for work, or one more productive than the present. A reasonable number of men are at work in all the bars, and invariably doing well. Many are making "big money" and probably not a single claim is being worked that does not pay. The stream is very low, and consequently easily managed. Less than half the labor is necessary to dam or turn the creek this season than in any previous summer since the settlement of the country.*[30]

In 1866, James Ovando Hollister, editor of the Central City newspaper (*The Register*) and author of *Mines of Colorado*, reported that the veins west of Idaho Springs were "...all on the south side of the creek and coming down very near the mill were under claim and being worked. Messrs. Thatch & Kinkead owned a 12-stamp water mill here, in good repair, and 3,000 feet of tunnels on the Cook, Anoka County, Phoenix, and Newcastle Lodes."[31]

The Idaho Springs area had sprouted mines like gopher holes in a potato patch. To connect them, the first true road, a toll road, came from Central City down Virginia Cañon into Idaho Springs by 1861. In 1866, Bayard Taylor, the great travel writer for the *New York Herald Tribune*, described Idaho Springs as he entered the valley from the original "Oh My God! Road."

We came upon a straggling village of log-huts, which, after having out-lived a variety of names, is now called "Idaho," — the inhabitants fondly supposing that this word means "the gem of the mountains." (I need hardly say that the Indians have no such phrase. Idaho is believed to mean "rocks.") In this queer, almost aboriginal village, with its charming situation, there is the best hotel in Colorado. It has just been completed; the opening ball occurred after I reached Central City. The astonished stranger here finds a parlor with carpets as showy, horse-hair sofas as shiny and slippery, looking-glasses with as much gilding, tables as marbled-topped, and everything else as radiant with varnish or gypsum, as the laws of American taste in such things could require. The bedrooms are so fresh — so unsuggestive of a thousand unwashed previous occupants — that I regretted not being able to enjoy the luxury for one night.

Where did Taylor not stay? The soon-to-be world-renowned Beebe House had just opened, located where the Elks Club is today. Other important guests during the forty-year duration of this five-star hotel included President Grant on his tour of the West in 1873. F.W. Beebe, owner of the Beebe House, was secretary/treasurer of the Virginia Cañon toll road; thus all stages stopped at his elegant hotel.

"A ride down Virginia Cañon... in one of the six-horse coaches of the Colorado Stage Company — the horses at full trot — is thrilling in the extreme," stated a Colorado promoter in 1871.[32] Two years later, President Grant's daughter, Nellie, was NOT thrilled with the white-knuckle stage-coach ride provided by famous stagecoach driver, Hiram (Hy) Washburn down the Virginia Cañon Road.

In its old age, the Beebe House was eventually separated into two buildings and the structures, now perhaps the oldest pieces remaining of an early hotel in Colorado, were moved east of the huge stone building called "The Castle," where they now serve as homes.[33]

President Grant and family in front of the Beebe House, 1873 (Courtesy Historical Society of Idaho Springs)

By 1867, Idaho Springs had another booster. Joel Parker Whitney, a shipping magnate from Boston, was entranced with Colorado's hidden silver wealth. During his first visit to the Territory in 1865, he narrowly escaped being robbed and murdered along the Virginia Cañon Road. The man following him wasn't as lucky.

At Spanish Bar, about 5 miles from Central, I was headed to visit my two friends, Brune and Davis, to enjoy fishing with them. Leading down to the Bar was a long steep ravine, called Virginia Cañon, which has a wagon road down it. Three-quarters of the way down was a deserted log cabin and a turn in the ravine. I met no one until I reached the cabin, and here I met a very rough man, hatless, whose countenance indicated the free use of ardent spirits and whose eyes were red from recent libations. He wore a thin linen coat, and as the breeze down the ravine blew it open, I saw that he was doubly armed with a brace of big six-shooters. I had met one of the double-pistol brigade, and it was not very pleasant, considering the place. I passed the word of day with him and kept on, declined the apparent disposition he seemed to evince for a parley. I was suspicious and as I kept on I slightly turned my head so as to keep him in view, and I saw that he had stopped and was regarding me, and he called out, asking if I had met anyone before him as I came down, to which I answered "NO," still keeping on, as I observed his right hand was on his pistol handle, where mine went without delay, as I was armed, and I kept steadily on, still keeping him in view and left him standing where he stopped, and the turn in the road soon left him out of view. I had not gone far — perhaps 20 rods — when I heard a pistol shot ring out from the place I had left him, but being quite out of range I presumed that in the half-maudlin state he was in he perhaps had taken a stray shot at one of the red squirrels which were plentiful along the ravine.

When I arrived at Brune's I told him of the occurrence, and he said the man was one of the bushwhackers who belonged to a gang which was camped up the stream a mile or so above, and that the chap had passed the house not long before and had stopped to ask for a drink which could not be furnished... After supper a man entered our cabin with a lantern, being a neighbor, saying that he had just come down the canyon and that there was a dead man lying in the road not far above the bend, who had evidently been shot and robbed, judging from the loose papers lying about him. Our glances were significant, and we saw that the man following me had been shot and robbed. We got two or three men to accompany us and all went up there, and found the dead man lying on his back as left in the road, with his face upturned and as placid in the full moonlight as if sleeping. Near, on the side of the road, where it had been carelessly thrown, was a long breast pocketbook, which had been stripped and from

The Virginia Cañon Road in Idaho Springs, 7/23/1899, Teitzel photo (Courtesy Historical Society of Idaho Springs)

which the loose papers had been thrown out... we rigged up some boards from the floor of the old cabin, carried him down to the Bar, depositing the body in an adjacent shed, and hunted up the Assistant Sheriff, who declined to go after the murderer that night, but would in the morning, and did, but found no trace of him and the matter was dropped.

The murdered man had no name or papers about him by which he could be identified... only two or three besides our party attended the burial. Brune got out his old Episcopal prayer-book and read the burial service. As he was reading, down the road came a dozen bushwhackers riding as if in a race. When they saw us on the hillside they abated the speed of their horses and came up to us, inquiring what was going on, and on being informed, one of them dismounted and, giving his horse in charge of a companion, said: "I will make a prayer for the dead man," and kneeling by the grave, gave a frightfully blasphemous prayer for the dead, remarking as he remounted, "That will save him from hell." They all then rode off at a racing speed and we saw no more of them. We remained silent during the interruption, and afterward Brune proceeded with the service.[34]

As the Colorado Territory commissioner to the Paris Universal Exposition of 1867, Whitney had purchased a collection of Colorado ores originally amassed by Henry Dewitt Clinton Cowles of Empire City. Cowles had displayed the collection at the Mechanics Fair in Boston in 1865. Whitney offered to take the collection, have maps and graphs of the mines of the Territory drafted, design a display complete with a detailed guidebook to Colorado's mines, and ship it all to Paris for the Exposition. Such a load of spectacular ore the world had never seen! Because Cowles was from Empire City, many of these chunks of valuable rock came from the mines along Clear Creek. The Cook, Edgar, Grundy Co., Harshaw, Hukill, Lincoln, Pike County, Pleasant Valley, Quail, Spanish, Silver Creek, "Sailsbury" (Hollister's spelling of Salisbury), and the Whale all provided samples for this grand exhibit.[35]

The frontispieces in the gold-bound display guidebook included beautiful foldout maps of the United States and Colorado Territory, plus a photograph of the display in a second edition of the fair book. The photograph shows a huge map on the left side of the display of Clear Creek County, one of the first ever made. This display exhibited maps of Colorado mines and mining districts. High-tech photographs framed in black walnut of Colorado scenery and mines lined the showcase. Stacks of gold and silver bullion graced the center display. Colorado Territory became the topic of everyone's conversation! The display won a gold medal and special commendation from Napoleon III.

The Colorado Room at the Paris Exposition, 1867 (From Whitney, 1867, Simmons collection)

The map of Clear Creek County now hangs in the Clear Creek County Archives. Some of the thousands of ore samples that went to Paris from around Central City are in the Gilpin County Museum.

CHAPTER THREE

Investors Come to Town

P rospectors found ore and staked their claims, then they sold the claims to miners or mining companies with the money to improve the land, develop the mines and build mills to process the ore. In the late 1860s, America was in a post-war depression. Joel Parker Whitney and a mining engineer named Robert Old, who oversaw the Colorado and British Mining Bureau, convinced many European investors to sink their money into the gold mines of eastern Clear Creek County.

The Colorado and British Mining Bureau was a clearinghouse for investors. Robert Old advocated investing in many of the mines around Idaho Springs. Specimens from the Star Lode, Goodenough, Whale, New, Fairmount, and other mines in the Spanish Bar District graced the shelves of the bureau office in London.[36] Money came in, rocks went out. At that time the ore was shipped across the country and sea to Swansea, Wales, where there was a great smelter.

In Colorado, mining technicians had been unsuccessfully trying to develop a profitable method of treating the sulfur-rich ores. In 1867, a chemist from Brown University, Nathaniel P. Hill, found the solution in Swansea, Wales. Hill then built the first commercial, successful smelter in Black Hawk. The ores still needed further refinement, so they were still shipped to Swansea for final separation until 1873. Hill further improved his techniques, and from that time on all smelting and metal recovery took place in Colorado.

Hill's partner, Richard Pearce, built one of the first successful, but short-lived, smelters in Clear Creek County at Empire Junction near the site of the old slaughterhouse cabin at Douglas Mountain. He used the immense pile of animal bones outside of the cabin's ruins as the bone ash base for his cupel assay cups.[37]

By 1880, Clear Creek County was a busy mining, manufacturing, and milling center of the country. The railroad had blasted its way along the base of the crags of spectacular Clear Creek Canyon, opening the mountains to invasions of *travelers, tourists, (of all sort and conditions) commercial drummers, scientific bug hunters, pleasure seekers, and possibly capitalists now and then.*[38]

The mountain towns were in their heyday. People came from far and near to see the wonders of the mines and the spectacular scenery from viewpoints such as Bellevue Mountain. For $2.50 to $3 a day, they rented horses, or for $10, a team with buggy to drive up to Chicago Lakes.[39] From there the "pleasure seekers" hiked up to the cirques of the great mountain now called Mount Evans. Even Albert Bierstadt, the great artist, memorialized the scenery of Clear Creek County in his famous painting, "Storm in the Rockies," which he created while at Chicago Lakes. Unfortunately, this

The Road up Berthoud Pass, 1920, Sanborn photo (Courtesy Historical Society of Idaho Springs)

painting never appeared in Paris at the 1867 Exposition. Apparently it got left on the loading dock in New York.[40]

The railroad developed after years of brainstorming. Renowned engineer Edwin L. Berthoud, outlined a route through Clear Creek County as early as 1861, when Jim Bridger told him about the pass called Berthoud which is crossed today by U.S. 40. In 1866, Taylor proposed a tunnel under Berthoud Pass to accommodate a railroad to Middle Park.

By February 24, 1873, the Colorado Central, using narrow-gauge track, had come up Clear Creek as far as Floyd Hill. The station was at the bottom of the hill, where Kermit's Saloon is today. From there, passengers took a stagecoach to Idaho Springs and points west.[41]

Legalities and political shenanigans delayed pushing the railroad farther up the canyon until 1877, when the Union Pacific reigned supreme in the railroad wars. By June 14, 1877, the train had reached Idaho Springs. In August of that year, the locomotive whistle on the Clear Creek Line was finally heard in Georgetown.[42]

In the summer of 1877, the fares to ride the "most daring railroad in the world" ranged from $3.55 for a three-day pass to $4 for a seven-day excursion ticket to Idaho Springs and back to Denver.[43] The railroad served as the main link between Clear Creek County and the outside world for almost fifty years.[44]

The Mount Vernon/Floyd Hill wagon road wasn't made an official automobile highway until the 1920s. U.S. 40 was routed over Berthoud Pass in the 1930s, the first national highway to cross the Continental Divide.

Early in World War II, the railroad went defunct and later the federal government opted to use the well-graded railroad bed for the base of a new highway through the dramatic canyon. Shortly after the railroad tracks were torn up and sold for scrap for the war effort, tunnels were bored through the rock, making a straighter, easier route for truckloads of ore coming from the URAD Molybdenum Mine and the other mines of Clear Creek County to reach the smelters in Denver. From Idaho Springs, passengers who didn't own automobiles could ride the Greyhound bus to anywhere in the country. The mountains were finally flung open to the world.

CHAPTER FOUR

Major Mines

The Colorado Mineral Belt is world-renowned for huge deposits of almost every metal known. The twenty-mile-wide "belt" stretches diagonally across the state from Boulder to the San Juan Mountains. The veins around Idaho Springs were very rich, producing millions of dollars of copper, gold, lead, molybdenum, silver, uranium, and zinc over the years.

The Colorado veins usually occur as fissure fillings of metals chemically combined with sulfur to form sulfide ores. Copper is commonly associated with gold; silver with lead. Named "auriferous pyrite" or "argentiferous galena," these common ores require heat treatment to chemically release the precious metals.

Over vast periods of time, rain and microorganisms released the metals near the surface, so the shallow ore deposits become "enriched." The prospectors looked for veins rich in gossan, rock that is a rusty red color with specks of gold dotting the surface. Assays on enriched veins are as great as twenty ounces per ton of gold ore; below the enriched zone, the assays on the same vein may be only one or two ounces per ton.

The veins (lodes) around Idaho Springs were discovered in 1860. They have been mined continuously since that time and new veins are still being discovered. The majority of the lodes are parallel bands oriented northeast to southwest that dip into the earth toward the northwest. The minerals filled old cracks in the earth's crust when hot fluids rose around local volcanoes that dotted the mountains as late as 26 million years ago.

Drifts, adits, shafts, winzes, and stopes, all workings from which ore or rock has been extracted, honeycomb the mountains. Miners are optimistic that less than half of the deposits in these old veins have been exploited.

An unusual deposit of the rare metal molybdenum, used to strengthen steel and lubricate machinery, occurs under Red Mountain, west of Empire, southwest of Berthoud Pass. Discovered in the early 1900s,[45] the URAD mine stripped the west side of this scenic glacial horn. After World War II, mining geologists discovered a rich, deeply buried deposit called the Henderson Stock, the remains of an ancient volcano that erupted about 29 million years ago. Mining the Henderson Stock has challenged mining engineers to remove the metal in this deep mine using the most environmentally friendly techniques they can create.[46] The Henderson Mine provides employment for most of today's miners in Clear Creek County.

The mines of eastern Clear Creek County, mostly gold producers, are world famous. The most productive over the 150 years since mining began have been the Lamartine and Freeland, up Trail Creek; the Alma-Lincoln and Stanley, along Clear Creek; the Gem and Franklin, accessible through the Argo Tunnel; the Dixie, up Ute Creek; the Black Eagle, up Chicago

Creek; the Alice, up Fall River; and the Champion and Specie Payment, on the southwestern slope of Bellevue Mountain. These are some of the mines that financed the entire nation during the late 1800s.

Another famous mine, the Edgar, is not renowned for its production (mostly silver), but rather for its role in training miners and rescue teams. Its huge drifts and stopes penetrate hundreds of feet into the mountain and provide testing sites where mine development companies can perfect patents; students from the Colorado School of Mines can practice drilling and blasting; and mine rescue teams from around the world can simulate real-life emergencies.

Most mines started out as independent claims, but mining magnates like John Dumont purchased claim upon claim, putting together parcels that could be more profitably mined and milled. Dumont, for whom the village of Dumont is named, created the Stanley, Fall River, and Freeland mining centers. The old company hotel and office building still stands along old U.S. Route 6, now the Stanley Road near the Stanley Mine.

Dumont made a fortune by selling these huge parcels to outside companies that could afford the financial outlay necessary to build the mills to treat the ore. British investors bought the Stanley, and Californian William MacKay purchased the Freeland.[47] The companies or lessees worked the mines until Government Order L208 closed the gold-producing mines in 1942.

The rules regulating mining claims originated in the local mining camps, where, in a truly democratic system, every claimant — man, woman,[48] and youth older than age 10, had equal say in the operation of the camp.[49] In 1872, because a great deal of mining occurred on federally owned land, the government passed the defining law that now regulates mining legalities. The Mining Law of 1872, written by mining lawyers and miners, is one of few that have withstood the test of time. Despite repeated lawsuits in opposition, the U.S. Supreme Court has never overruled it.[50]

In 1892, Colorado passed a tunneling law that allowed companies to drill into the mountains to intersect the veins at depth. Individual mine owners along the route paid to use the tunnel for transportation to the mill for drainage, and to run air and water lines to their mines. This system greatly reduced expenses, because the miners no longer had to sink shafts and hoist ore and water to the surface of their claim.[51]

Funded by loyal, royal British fans, Samuel Newhouse quickly set about driving his tunnel (now called the Argo) north under Seaton and Pewabic Mountains toward Central City. Other tunnels included the Rockford, under the Trail Creek District; the Monarch (or McClelland), accessing the Freeland mines; the Burns-Moore, aiming for the Lamartine veins under Alps Mountain; and the Lucania, under Bellevue Mountain. Rees Vidler tried to cross under the Continental Divide with his Vidler Tunnel[52] at East

Argentine, a ghost town high in the mountains above Georgetown. He would be delighted to know that his efforts have paid off — water now flows through his tunnel under the Divide to cities on the eastern slopes.

STANLEY MINE

West of Idaho Springs, along old Route 6, is the mine with the longest history that visitors can easily see — the Stanley. Initially filed on as independent veins, the Whale and the Hukill, the early lodes proved to be one and the same. Dumont merged the claims and added others that crossed the hills on both sides of Clear Creek into the Consolidated Stanley. He sank the Gehrman Shaft, over which now sits the huge, old, yellow, metal-sided shaft house along Clear Creek.[53]

The Stanley in its heyday, 1910 (Courtesy Historical Society of Idaho Springs)

The Stanley Mine produced over $3.5 million (worth $67 million in the twenty-first century) before 1900. The last miner to work in the Stanley was Cliff Morrison, who leased the mine in the 1970s. He died in a cave-in working in the mine's dark hollowed tunnels. The yellow buildings stand as proud remnants of the great gilded age of gold mining in Idaho Springs.

THE ALMA-LINCOLN MINE

Just west of the Stanley, a huge mine dump covers the mountainside. These are the remains of the consolidated mine group called the Alma-Lincoln. Drifts and mine shafts penetrate into the mountainside south of Clear Creek, chasing the elusive Lincoln, Josephine, and Elliot-Barber veins. This group of mines was worked steadily over the years, providing much-needed employment during the Great Depression.[54]

Looking west at the Alma Lincoln, c.1872 (Courtesy Historical Society of Idaho Springs)

The Alma Lincoln, 1908 (USGS Professional Paper #63, plate 76A)

The buildings on the site are now mere skeletons of previous structures of the operation, but the mine dump hasn't changed much since the turn of the twentieth century.

TRAIL CREEK AND RUN DISTRICTS

The rich lodes of Trail Creek lie southwest of the Stanley group. They were originally set out as two separate mining districts, Trail Creek and Trail Run.

The Freeland was the first lode found by a man named Freeland. He, like others following him, abandoned it. Then, Israel Stotts bought the claim and began developing it. He established the little mining settlement of Trail Run Camp, known today as Freeland.

Eventually Stotts sold the claim to John Dumont, who purchased many patented and unpatented claims and formed the Freeland Mining Company. Dumont developed and then sold the productive Freeland to William MacKay in 1879. But Dumont retained placer claims, water rights, and a lode called the Lone Tree farther up the valley.

By the 1880s, the Freeland, using MacKay's money, boasted the largest gold mill in Colorado.[55] Its likeness graced volumes of major history and travel books, complete with underground maps of the three levels of the mine and its many stopes.[56] Several large mine dumps are all that remain of this great enterprise.

One of the mines of the Freeland District was appropriately called the "Amethyst," from the beautiful doubly terminated purple quartz crystals in its vugs. Some were very large and were faceted into gemstones. One is in the Smithsonian Institution Gem Collection.

The waves of the Civil War in the East washed all the way to Colorado Territory. During the earliest days of the war (the late fall of 1861) Southerners William Green and Dr. Levi Oliver Russell often had their flumes cut at night by northern sympathizers. These channels brought much needed water through the Consolidated Ditch from the Fall River to Russell Gulch in nearby Gilpin County. Alexander Hunt, marshal of Colorado Territory, had to quell a "rabble" at the Russell Gulch mines, during which the Union rousers took over the mines and threatened the Russell brothers if they interfered. Hunt, a friend of the Russells, managed to reestablish peace in Russell Gulch. Such incidents sparked the Russells to head home toward Georgia the following spring in a trek that altered their families' lives forever. Only William Green Russell ever returned to Colorado.[57]

The Amethyst Mine was the center of the only Civil War fracas in Clear Creek County. In 1862, James Peck and his son, Frank, had moved over to Trail Creek in Clear Creek County, from Whitcomb, better known now as Nevadaville. There Peck had managed the Whitcomb Mill, an old Spanish arrastra operated by ox-power. In Trail Run, James Peck took charge of the Van Dearn Mill, owned by Joseph Cooley. Peck worked ore from the

Amethyst lode. Robert Tennel, an outspoken southern sympathizer, whose organization was known as the "Secesh gang," also worked ore from the Amethyst, which he eventually purchased and called the Tennel Mine,[58] in his Sears mill.[59]

Trail Creek had a reputation as the "worst rebel hole" in the territory. The rift between the northern and southern factions working there widened and split when Fred Brown, representing the Cooley interests, notified Colonel Leavenworth in the spring of 1862 that Trail Creek rebels were threatening the camp.[60]

Colonel Leavenworth responded with a detachment of the Third Colorado Regiment. He arrested Hyram G. Merrick, R.B. Griswold, D. D. Delarchmont, B.F. Gorby, George W. Bayliss, and two or three others. Several men who had been guarding the Tennel Mine escaped to the hills. Enroute to Empire City, where they spent the night, Colonel Leavenworth offered his prisoners an opportunity to escape, which they declined. But, feelings at Empire City were running high against the prisoners and no food could be obtained for them there. So the next day they were marched to Mill City, where a preliminary hearing was held. Some of the prisoners were bound over to trial in Clear Creek County. One of the local men who had been arrested, Hyram G. Merrick, was accepted as their bondsman. But the case was never prosecuted.

It turned out that George W. Bayliss, one of the arrested men, was a Union spy! Ordered to Trail Creek to investigate the movements of southern sympathizers, Bayliss had assumed the character of a southerner with so much enthusiasm that he seemed the most rampant "rebel" in the camp. He learned that there was a secret organization with a rendezvous "below Denver" that was enlisting soldiers for the South. He reported the case to Governor Gilpin, who arrested all of the men who had enlisted.[61]

After this fracas, James Peck wearied of the warfare at Trail Creek. Although he had staked out claims in Trail Run, he decided to move west to the staunch northern stronghold of Empire City, in the Union Mining District, where he became "the emperor of Empire."[62]

This was probably the last real excitement to ever occur along Trail Creek.

LAMARTINE MINE

The Lamartine was probably the most productive gold mine in all of Clear Creek County's history. Originally staked by four prospectors, the mine passed into the hands of Peter Himrod through his sister, a widow of one of the original four claimants. Himrod, who had come to Colorado on a health-seeking mission, bought out the other claimants and hired a prospector who discovered a hidden vein about 100 feet below the surface of Alps Mountain. Unfortunately, Peter Himrod died before he could

The Lamartine, c. 1915, McLean photo (Courtesy Patricia Mosch)

benefit from the discovery, but his son, Peter Junior, took Silas Hanchett from Empire and three other local miners in as partners and lessees to develop the mine. In less than two years, the immense vein produced gold worth over $616,000 (worth $11,900,000 in the twenty-first century). Crude estimates put the total production of the Lamartine at $7 million (worth $45 million in the twenty-first century) since 1890. This does not take into account the amount that was high graded from a huge pocket of pure gold found by the miners in the 1920s.[63]

The mine was worked intermittently into the 1950s. Each company that owned it improved the buildings, erected new mills, and drove even more tunnels. The length of drifts and other workings in the Lamartine system is estimated to be more than twelve miles.

FALL RIVER MINES

The mines north of Clear Creek were also good producers. The Fall River "debouches" into Clear Creek[64] about three miles west of Idaho Springs. It is one of the few places in the country where a river is tributary to a creek! Farther to the west, another "river," the "Roaring River," "debouched" into the West Branch of Clear Creek off the face of Quartz Mountain west of Empire. Because "he maintained he had never seen nor heard of a river emptying into a creek," local property owner Paul Lindstrom renamed it Mad Creek for its unpredictable behavior.[65]

The Spanish Bar, the great gold-bearing sand and gravel bar between the mouth of the Fall River and Idaho Springs, gave hints of the wealth that lay upstream. William Green Russell and George Jackson visited these sites in 1858 and 1859,[66] respectively.

Early prospectors worked glacial and stream placer deposits in the 1860s and recovered some silver ore at the camp, which was called Silver City. However, the value of the ores in the Fall River Districts wasn't recognized until the 1870s.

High above the confluence of the streams, on the southwestern slope of Bellevue Mountain, sit the three mine dumps of the Specie Payment. This multiple-drift mine opened in 1876. Visible gold often occurred in the ore, flecked or spotted on white quartz. In 1877, the mine owners built a fifteen-stamp mill in Idaho Springs to process the rich ore.

Even higher than the Specie Payment was the Champion. A great aerial tram that ran like a ski lift carried buckets up and down the mountain to the Champion mine. The miners rode it to and from their work. At the large Donelson Mill located at the mouth of the Fall River, a crusher, stamps, rolls, jigs, and amalgamation plates processed the ores.[67] A second aerial tram crossed Clear Creek, carrying ore from the Kelly-Donaldson Mine high on the hill to the south, above Trail Run.

In 1867 Hollister, author of *The Mines of Colorado*, reported that the Fall River District included the Iowa, Lower Fall River, Lincoln, Cumberland, and Upper Fall River Mining District, in today's Alice area. Hollister described the mining operation on the "right bank, easily accessible and open to the sun, as regularly pitted with prospect holes as a harvested potato patch. He estimated that 1500 claims had been made on 'yellow dirt.' "[68]

J.M. Dumont, the mover and shaker of this district, also managed the lodes of the Equitable Gold Mining Company. Dumont opened an adit on the Calendar vein and a tunnel 400 feet above it, aiming to cross the Wilson, Chicago, Noye , Red, and New Lodes, all which came to the surface. He built a dam to supply "600 feet of waterpower with a 24-foot fall, abreast of the lodes"[69] and was preparing to build a mill in 1867. Just above the Calendar project, Dumont tunneled into the mountainside, aiming for the Jones, Cook County, Advent, Briggs, Red, Cedar, and OK veins that had been claimed on the surface. Along the same sunny hillside, Samuel Cushman of Central City sold stock in the Fall River Mining Company which had been organized in 1864. Their tunnel went in 100 feet. Their adit on the Pulaski lode showed that the vein pinched out. The Fall River Mining Company had a "dwelling house" but no mill or machinery.[70]

The Montrose Gold Company of Colorado mined the Phillips, mostly a placer mine, the Almy, the Buffalo, and twenty other lodes. J. G. Mahany was the agent for this company, which owned an eighteen-stamp mill with four or five Dodge pans in a building 40 x 94 feet with a wheel house 20 x 36 feet. There was a two-story dwelling 20 x 30 feet with a 13 x 23 feet wing, a well-finished boarding house large enough for forty miners, a barn, a blacksmith shop, and other outbuildings. The waterpower for this operation came through a sluice 1,000 feet in length with a fifty-foot fall.[71]

Miners knew there was an easier way to move the ore, so they excavated great tunnels under Bellevue Mountain. Expanded by Mark Stapleton in the 1950s, the Lucania Tunnel now extends over 8,000 feet to Russell Gulch, intersecting many veins.

Ten miles farther, at the upper end of the road, placers in the Alice District were claimed as early as 1860. By 1867, The Union Company which mined the Hardup lode, had a shaft 127-feet deep with two feet of gold ore that assayed $279 a ton. Their surface facilities included a twelve-stamp steam mill with a 25-horsepower engine and water flume 500 feet long. There was another eight-stamp mill in the same area, perhaps serving the McClelland Mine. The McClelland's two shafts, 45- and 60-feet deep, mined a vein of ore that averaged eighteen inches and assayed $300 a ton. The Sullivan had four shafts from 25- to 50-feet deep, "good dirt and quartz crevice, prospecting rich."[72] By 1867, a good deal of work had been done on the Ross lode where it crossed the perpendicular mountainside, "with one edge of the ore crevice forever covered with snow." [73]

Hollister thus made the first mention in the literature of what is now called St. Mary's Glacier and St. Mary's Lake. He portrayed Mary's Lode, like the Ross, as plunging 200 yards down the face of the mountain into Mary's Lake, "a sheet of water of five or six acres," the headwaters of the "right fork of the river."[74] When Mary was canonized is not known.

Hydraulic mining started in 1881 and produced about $50,000 worth of gold,[75] $12,000 alone in 1884.[76] Colonel A.J. Cropsey of Nebraska, the superintendent of the Alice Mining Company, was banking between $1,200-$1,500 every two weeks in the First National Bank at Central City. The summer and fall production was so successful that the following February the capital stock of the company increased from $1 million to $2 million. Another ditch brought in water for hydraulic mining. Log cabins and a mill were built. The road was improved and the company banked $2,500 to $3,000 every two weeks.

The Alice Mine and other properties sold for $225,000 in 1897. The new owners planned to enlarge the 200-ton concentrator mill and initiate large air drills to mine the lode. However, in 1899, about the time the last payment on the loan was due, the mines closed.[77]

Two mills were operating in Alice in 1911, the Anchor and the Princess Alice, processing ores from six mines.[78] During the 1930s, the increase in the fixed price of gold from $20 to $35 per ounce saw a rebirth of Alice. The log cabins came back to life, and the new mill started to work ore that was mined using the new "glory hole" technique.[79] The monzonite ores of the Alice Mine — full of spectacular pyrite, sphalerite, and quartz crystals — were similar to the massive stock work of the Patch Mine near Central City.

Glory hole mining involves blasting the ore loose from underneath and letting it drop into open stopes within the mountain. Then the ore is mucked out and carted to the mill on the lower level. Citing environmental concerns, the United States Environmental Protection Agency filled the 150-foot-deep Alice Glory Hole in the 1970s.[80]

VIRGINIA CANYON MINES

Both the Fall River Valley and Virginia Canyon served as pathways for early roads to Central City. Many of the veins that cross the canyon were among the first hard rock mines opened in the county. Most of the mines access the Seaton Vein, the first silver vein found in Colorado.

Colonel A.R. Seaton of Kentucky discovered the Seaton Mine on Seaton Mountain on July 4, 1860. The ore was sent by oxen teams to St. Joseph, Missouri, on to New York by rail, and from there by ship to Wales for processing. In spring of 1867, Nathaniel P. Hill constructed the Boston and Colorado Smelter in Black Hawk. The ore was then milled at Idaho Springs, near Chicago Creek, and the concentrates were shipped to Black Hawk for smelting.

The Seaton shaft is over 400-feet deep and served six mine levels. One stope in the Seaton was reportedly 380-feet long and over 300-feet high. In 1903, the mine averaged 300 to 400 tons per month, requiring a work force of about forty men. From the Seaton's deepest level, the sixth, the mine finally connected with the Foxhall Tunnel, or seventh level, and ore was then mined through this second lower portal.

In 1906, the Seaton Mine had a shaft house with a gallows frame, a blacksmith shop, a carpenter shop, and a horse stable at the shaft collar. A second blacksmith shop, a carpenter shop, a bunkhouse with an office and storerooms, a powderhouse, and ore bins were located at the Foxhall Tunnel below the Seaton Mine.

The Seaton was one of the more valuable properties in the county; it was worked steadily from 1860 to 1872 and then intermittently until 1922. It was the first Colorado mine that changed from rich gold ore at the surface to rich silver ore at depth. Before 1899, the Seaton had produced $600,000 worth of metals. Between 1902 and 1922, based on 1986 metal prices, it produced over $6.4 million. Six thousand tons of smelting ore shipped in 1902 contained 9,000 ounces of gold. The Seaton vein was also mined through the Argo Tunnel in Idaho Springs at a vertical depth of 1,200 feet, where it also had rich ore.

About halfway up the face of Seaton mountain, the Comstock, named after the famous Nevada gold mine, produced over $200,000 in gold and silver ore prior to 1889. The Dove's Nest Mine had a 600-foot inclined shaft, six levels, and about 1,000 feet of "drifts" (horizontal mine workings that follow veins). It was originally discovered in May 1879. Production was $350,000 prior to 1900, which included over 1,500 ounces of gold and 20,000 ounces of silver produced in just four years. This mine became the focus of a lengthy lawsuit, as did many of the rich mines in the county. Lawyers received much of the profits.

On the higher portion of the Virginia Canyon Road are the modern buildings of the Two Brothers Mine, last operated by Dr. Fred Metz, a great dental-implant inventor and a second-generation resident in Idaho Springs. It connects with the Bald Eagle shaft, which opens even higher on the southeastern side of Bellevue Mountain.

CHICAGO CREEK MINES

Chicago Creek follows a great fault zone. There is little mineralization on the eastern side of the fault, but on the western side, the ore bodies are some of the richest in Clear Creek County. Tributaries of Chicago Creek that head on Alps Mountain cut across many of the veins.

Lord Bryon Shaft House, c. 1900, Teitzel photo (Courtesy Historical Society of Idaho Springs)

Starting at the mouth of Chicago Creek, just behind Jackson's Bar, were the Waltham Mine and Mill. Upstream was the Black Eagle, once connected to its mill on the opposite side of the creek by an aerial tramway.[81] In the 1970s the mill was renovated with a ball mill, jigs, classifiers, and flotation tanks. Vacuum filters dried the slurry, which was then loaded onto trucks for the trip to Golden. There, the ore was loaded on a train for shipment to the ASARCO smelters either in Amarillo or El Paso, Texas, depending on their content.[82]

The Jewelry Shop Mine along Chicago Creek above the mouth of Spring Gulch wasn't discovered until the 1920s. Rich in telluride ores, it produced ore throughout the Depression. Further upstream was the rich, long-producing Little Mattie Mine.

The veins that cross Spring Gulch were very rich. The Lord Byron and the Kitty Clyde in the upper part of the valley, the Torpedo and the Skyrocket Veins all produced high-grade gold ore.[83] A rich silver lode in Cascade Creek, called the Charter Oak, was worked for many years.

Treasures abounded in mines of Ute Creek, including the Humboldt and the Dixie.[84] The Dixie was the richest mine on Ute Creek and perhaps in Clear Creek County. Much of the gold in the Dixie was "free," occurring in beautiful flakes, crystals, and wires, now highly coveted by mineral

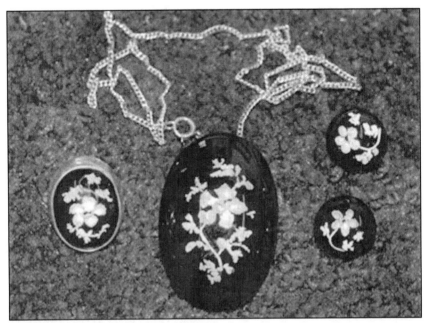

Dixie Mine jewelry, 2004, Don Allan photo (Courtesy Historical Society of Idaho Springs)

collectors. During the 1940s, LeRoy Giles and Company, owners of the lucrative Dixie, purchased the old Dixie Mill at Hidden Valley along Clear Creek.

One of the most interesting sidelines of Idaho Springs gold mining was a unique line of jewelry that local jewelers created. Gold flakes and wires, arranged into intricate designs of flowers and other shapes, were cast into Lucite mountings with a black background. The beautiful creations were set into spectacular rings, brooches, and other jewelry[85] and sold through the curio shop in the Dixie mill. These are highly coveted pieces in Idaho Springs.

Gold mines are still being discovered in Clear Creek County. In 1974, fourteen-year old David Mosch — with help from his sisters Cyndi and Sue — attained national acclaim when they found the presently-called gold-rich Resurrection Vein along Trail Creek near their parents' Phoenix Mine along Trail Creek Road.

CHAPTER FIVE

Mechanics in the Mountains

MILLS IN THE HILLS

I daho Springs grew by leaps and bounds during the late 1800s as a center for the mining industry. The waters of Clear Creek and surrounding streams provided power to run arrastras. Water also supplied steam engines and other equipment for more advanced mines and mills. By the turn of the century there had been hundreds of mills in Clear Creek County; at least twenty-five were in Idaho Springs alone.[86] Most of the mills used gravity-driven systems to move material through the processing cycle, ending at the creek level with finished concentrates ready to load into railroad cars.

Each mill had its function in the processing of gold ore. Some were assay sample mills, where the miners took the ore to be tested. Others were stamp mills, with or without amalgamation tables. As technology advanced, new processes quickly found their way to Clear Creek County mines and mills.

The first mill erected to process ore from the Hukill Mine in 1864 used the newest fad, a Brückner Cylinder.[87] The Brückner Cylinder was a huge

© Colorado Historical Society

The old Whale Mill, 1870, Reed & McKinney photo (Courtesy Colorado Historical Society #X-4592)

Wifley Table, Alma Lincoln Mill, 1940, Bob Zellers photo (Courtesy Colorado Historical Society #X-5494)

metal barrel twelve feet long and five feet in diameter, lined with firebrick that rotated like a barbecue. The ore would be charged into the furnace through a hopper and mixed with the fuel, usually wood. Then the machine was fired up and set to rotate, burning off up to 25 percent of the sulfur content. The gases emitted from the furnace rose into the clear skies above Clear Creek County.[88] The fancy cylinder did not work well on the refractory ores from the veins of Clear Creek, and the Colvin Gold Mining Company called it quits after two years, just before Nathaniel P. Hill built his smelter in nearby Gilpin County.[89]

Smelters separated the ore by melting the rock, but at a high cost. Railroads had to cart the required coal into the mountains from the beds that lay in the Laramie Formation along the Front Range. The trains met many obstacles, from rocks on the tracks to derailments during floods and rock falls. The mines and mills poured pollutants into the streams and air. Residents went to sleep and woke to the incessant rhythm of the stamp mills. However, in the 1880s, these were considered to be "signs of progress."

To save shipping costs, each mining center had a number of "concentration mills," where the ore was crushed and preprocessed before shipping to the smelter. During the early years, the mills were mostly stamp and amalgamation mills using the reciprocating energy of a steam engine to turn a camshaft with three, five, ten or more piston-shaped stamps on rods. After a Blake Jaw Crusher had broken the ore into small pieces, the stamps pulverized the ore.

In the early mills, the ore was washed with water over a copper-lined table coated with mercury (quicksilver). Liquid mercury attracted the gold as it sank into the liquid and formed a matte called "amalgam." Aware of the dangers of mercuric poisoning (Mad Hatter's Disease) inventors went to work and created huge "bumping" tables that worked like a gold pan. The heavy metals dropped out first as the solution of concentrates and water flowed across a jiggling table. The most commonly used was the Wifley table. The amalgam was then sent by railroad to the smelters in Black Hawk, Golden, or Denver.[90]

SMELTERS
There were a few small unsuccessful smelters in the Idaho Springs area. In 1882, angry over the cost of freighting on the railroad, John H. Dumont and George Vivian built the Bullion or Bonito Smelter[91] just upstream from the village of Freeland in its pretty little suburb called "affectionately"[92] "Bonito." Burning twenty-four cords of firewood daily to roast the concentrates, they treated 7,200 tons of ore but extracted little gold. All that remains today is a large, leveled pile of enriched black slag.

For a short time in the late 1800s, the Stanley Mine sported a smelter, but most of the concentrates were shipped to the huge Argo Smelter north of Denver or to other less known refractories in Denver or Golden. Later, during the twentieth century, concentrates were trucked to the smelter at Leadville.

CHEMICAL PROCESSES
In the 1880s, mills went through a phase of using the chlorination process, a complicated series of chemical steps that broke down the sulfide ores using chlorine gas. The process began with roasting the ore.[93] During this step, a wood fire that burned nonstop for two or three months heated huge heaps of ore. Imagine the odor as sulfide gases wafted into the air!

The advantages of using cyanide to leach gold ore were quickly proven in the Cripple Creek District in the 1890s; by the second decade of the 1900s, mills in Clear Creek County had adopted the process.[94] The leftover cyanide solution was dumped into Clear Creek where the turbulence of the water added oxygen that broke the cyanide into nitrogen and carbon within a short distance downstream. The additional nitrogen in the water nurtured the crops grown along Clear Creek valley's irrigated districts east of Golden.[95]

Then came flotation, a process using bubbles to carry heavy metals out of a solution.[96] Carrie Everson, wife of Chicago doctor William Knight

Flotation cells at the Alma Lincoln Mill, 1940, Bob Zellers photo (Courtesy Colorado Historical Society #X-5495)

Everson, both of whom were investors in the Golden Age Mining Company owned by "Brick" Pomeroy, were concerned about poor returns from the mine. Carrie, proficient in chemistry, tested a revolutionary process to separate metal from crushed fine rock in her husband's Chicago lab during the 1880s. On August 4, 1886, Carrie Everson received a patent for a process that used a solution of fats or oils to combine with metal particles and float off, leaving the waste behind.

Mrs. Everson visited Georgetown on August 5, 1886, and demonstrated the process. Because of her husband's untimely death, Carrie was unable to develop the idea into industrial scope, but her work laid the foundation for the modern "flotation" process now used throughout the milling industry.[97]

Carrie Everson's story became a now-debunked legend originally purported by Colorado State Geologist Thomas A. Rickard. In one of his reports, Rickard transformed Carrie Everson into a schoolteacher in Leadville who was washing her assayer brother's pants and noted the presence of gold particles on the bubbles in her laundry tub after she washed his clothes and sample bags. Rickard suggested that her womanhood left her ill equipped to deal with the technological development of the simple procedure![98]

Thomas Alva Edison worked on the flotation process in the Burleigh Mill near Silver Plume, but it took miners in New Zealand to perfect the process. Flotation was added to the chain of processes in the Argo Mill in 1916.[99]

MINING EQUIPMENT

A major technological advance in mining came in 1839 when the Singer brothers patented the first drop-drill. After the Civil War, the pneumatic drill was perfected and was used for the first time in the Burleigh Tunnel at Silver Plume in 1869. A piston driven by air pressure, the heavy device could drill ten times as fast as single- and double-jack man teams. However, it quickly earned the name of "widow maker" because the dust given off found its way into miners' lungs. Miners in Clear Creek County began dying off like flies from consumption otherwise known as silicosis.

Another important invention came out of France in the 1870s — the diamond drill. Used for core drilling, the diamond-tipped drill offered geologists the chance to examine the rocks at depth without the expense of driving a drift or sinking a shaft.[100]

John and Manser Puckert double-jacking at the Silver Leaf Mine, c. 1900, McLean photo (Courtesy Historical Society of Idaho Springs)

During the development of the Newhouse Tunnel in Idaho Springs, Denver inventor J.G. Leyner experimented with hollow drill bits made by boring the hole like a rifle barrel. Then he welded the drill bit to the end. In 1900, after many complaints from the miners about excessive dust, Leyner introduced his lifesaving wet pneumatic drill.[101]

By the end of the first decade of the twentieth century, drill engineers developed a machine now known as the "jumbo drill," capable of poking twelve holes into the breast of the tunnel at one time. [102] In the fifteen years of construction at the Newhouse Tunnel, miners worked through all of these technological changes while they penetrated

The Alma Lincoln horse-drawn ore tram, 1920 (Courtesy Denver Public Library Western History Collection #X-61667)

The Alma Lincoln electric-powered ore tram, 1940 (Courtesy Colorado Historical Society #X-5489)

21,000 feet under Seaton and Pewabic Mountains to create this new wonder of the world.

One of the largest drills used in Clear Creek County was a huge jumbo mounted on a rail, designed specifically for the Eisenhower Tunnel project on Interstate 70. The jumbo was a three-stage platform monster with twelve tungsten carbide steel bits, ten- and twelve- feet long, protruding from the front. Driven by compressed air, the bits cut twelve holes at once in the face of the tunnel. Water poured through the hollow drill bits to clean out the holes and saturate the rock dust.[103]

Another key development that aided mining was the invention of dynamite by Alfred Nobel in 1865.[104] No longer were miners susceptible to the unpredictable black powder and fuse. They could plant the charge of dynamite in the holes, light the sequence of fuses and then leave the face well before the blast. The danger lay in blasting caps that misfired and had to be doused with water and taken out by hand.[105]

The development of electricity was another boon to miners.[106] The first electric hoist was installed in the Veteran Tunnel in Aspen in 1888. Following that example, Clear Creek County mines soon had electric hoists and lights operating on alternating current as developed by the early electrical inventor Nicola Tesla. Soon after electrical wiring came the blasting box: using it, the miners could set off their charges from outside the mine. Electric trams quickly replaced horse- or mule-drawn ore trains, slashing the cost of mining and saving mens' and animals' lives.

In Idaho Springs, the Seaton (Gem) electric plant was on the east end of town. The Seaton Steam Generating Electrical Power Plant was in the middle of town, just east of the water wheel site today. William E. Renshaw managed both. On the west end of Idaho Springs, Lafayette Hanchett managed Cascade Electric, a branch of the Union Light and Power Company of Georgetown.[107]

Households were the last frontier of electrical application. Thanks to a pricing war between the two electric companies in Idaho Springs, homes were equipped with electric lights by 1903. However, electric stoves and refrigerators were not invented until after World War I. Visitors can observe one of the county's earliest hydropower plants (from 1900) still operating, at the Georgetown Energy Museum.

Technology also affected communications. The telegraph came with the railroad across the plains in the 1860s. Each train depot had a telegraph station, usually a busy place in towns such as Idaho Springs and Georgetown.

But soon a new-fangled invention called the telephone was carrying the human voice along wires across the mountains. By 1900, one of the first telephone lines in the county ran from Georgetown up Saxon Mountain to Lamartine, then down the Trail Run Canyon into Idaho Springs.[108] Anna

The Seaton Steam Generating Electrical Power Plant, 1902, Marchington Photo (Courtesy Historical Society of Idaho Springs)

McKinley, the operator in Idaho Springs, became the center of community communication.

Idaho Springs was a mining boomtown prior to World War I, after suffering a financial crash in 1911, just after the Newhouse Tunnel was completed.

During the 1920s, an interesting variety of galena called "steel galena" was sold from some of the mines in Clear Creek County. Prior to the easy availability of vacuum tubes by consumers, this galena was used in crystal radio sets. The crystal worked as a rectifier and was able to transform radio waves into sound waves. Tuning was accomplished by positioning the point of a very fine wire called a "cat whisker" to various spots on the crystal. Headphones were used to hear the audio messages.[109]

The first switchboard at Idaho Springs, Anna McKinley, operator, 1898 (Courtesy Denver Public Library Western History Collection #X-2338)

Mining and milling picked up in 1934 during the Great Depression, when the government raised the price of gold to thirty-five dollars per ounce. But in 1942, during World War II, Government Order L208 closed all gold and silver mines not producing at least seventy percent in lead, zinc, or other minerals necessary for the war. Mica, beryllium, uranium, molybdenum, and tungsten were key metals taken from Clear Creek County for the war effort.

Since World War II, the area has undergone extensive development as well as the construction and improvements to federal highways 6 and 40 and Interstate 70. Mining still continues on a large scale at the huge Henderson Molybdenum Mine at the head of the West Branch of Clear Creek. On a smaller scale, local miners develop old mines waiting for the price of gold to rise to profitable levels.

THE NEWHOUSE TUNNEL AND ARGO MILL

A tour through the old Argo Mill illustrates the immense size of the mills and their operations. The Argo Mill was built in 1912 to treat the ores brought through the Newhouse Tunnel, which is 4.16 miles long and extends northward beneath the Central City Mining District. The tunnel set the standard for a new pattern of underground cooperative mining, inspiring over 100 miles of tunnels in the greater Idaho Springs area alone.

Its construction initiated innovative techniques that became standard in tunnel development worldwide.[110]

Samuel Newhouse conceived the idea of building a tunnel from Central City to Idaho Springs that would drain the mines and provide easy access for the ore to a mill in Idaho Springs. The ore could then be shipped on the railroad to the smelters at the base of the mountains. Newhouse, "ever the dreamer and colorful character, a gentle man of most winsome and kindly nature, very persuasive in his arguments, prone to hasty judgments and by nature much inclined to do the bold and spectacular thing guided by the impulse of the moment formed the Argo Mining, Drainage, Transportation and Tunnel Company, primarily with English [i.e. Prince Edward's] backing."[111]

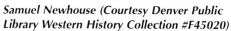

Samuel Newhouse (Courtesy Denver Public Library Western History Collection #F45020)

Newhouse started his tunnel in 1893. By March 1896, the *Mining and Scientific Press* reported that the Newhouse Tunnel had reached about 4,750 feet, penetrating 300 feet per month.[112] A. J. Ventress served as head surveyor for the project.[113]

In May of 1896, the *Mining and Scientific Press* described the drills used at the Newhouse Tunnel at Idaho Springs.

> ... *twelve feet in length. Nine holes are drilled in the breast of the tunnel for every charge. The charge of powder required for each blast is 400 pounds of Giant. The charge is fired from a battery in a recess a quarter of a mile distant. Nearly 200 tons of rock are broken down at every discharge, and half a day is required to clear away the debris after the shots are fired. The tunnel is 12 feet square and it has not been found necessary to do any timbering since solid formation was reached. The gases from the explosion are directed into the drainage trough and carried off in the water, so that there is the least possible delay in the work.*[114]

In November 1896, W. H. Smith and W. H. Wiley sank the first airshaft from the Edgardine Mine 600 feet to make the first air-hole connection with the Newhouse Tunnel. However, later in 1896, the railroad Newhouse was depending upon went bankrupt. Only 200 claim owners agreed to pay for the benefit of the tunnel.

In 1899, excavation ceased. Then, Newhouse persuaded another Idaho Springs soon-to-be-famous mine manager, Lafayette Hanchett, to prepare a report for the London money backers on the benefits of continuing the Newhouse Tunnel. The London people agreed to the deal, providing Hanchett managed the operation. Hanchett was the son of Silas Hanchett, the manager at the Lamartine Mine. When Silas took ill, twenty-two-year-old Lafayette had taken over his position. For a number of years, Lafayette Hanchett managed both the Newhouse operation and the Lamartine Mine.[115]

By January 1902, the tunnel was only halfway to Central City when a premature explosion killed the shift boss, A.C.B. Laws, and two workers — Ernest Wheeler and John Eckart. Harry Baird and Louis Phillips were seriously injured. Superintendent Silas Knowles had warned the men of the dangers and was not held responsible.[116]

The Newhouse project was completed under different ownership in 1908, and finally ore arrived from some of the twenty-eight mines that fed into the tunnel.[117] By 1910, the volume of ore being transported through the tunnel had become so large that stockholders decided to build their

The Newhouse Tunnel, 1900, Teitzel photo (Courtesy Historical Society of Idaho Springs)

Newhouse dump and power house, 1900, Teitzel photo (Courtesy Historical Society of Idaho Springs)

Miners inside the Newhouse with horse and air vent, 1900, Teitzel photo (Courtesy Historical Society of Idaho Springs)

own mill. The Argo Mill opened on April 1, 1913, as a custom stamp and concentrating mill to handle the ores coming through the Newhouse, by now called the Argo Tunnel.[118] This mill was the first to use electrical conveyor belts or chain buckets to move ore from place to place. The muck cars were emptied at the end of the dump. A car dumper called "the barrel" near the railroad track dumped four cars at one time into the bins filling the railroad cars on their way to the smelters in Denver.[119]

In 1917, the mill offered cyanidation and concentration processes that included the newest method, flotation, which had been added in 1916. The mill included a gyratory crusher, twenty 1,050-pound stamps, six Dorr classifiers, seven Dorr thickeners, nine Card tables, Parrall and Dorr agitators, and a Portland filter.[120]

Over the next twenty years the mill processed more than $100 million of low-grade ore — equal to over $1 billion in the twenty-first century — that would have otherwise remained in the ground.[121] By 1928, the completely modern 150-ton mill was adapted to treat any variety of ore found in the district. The flow could be switched from selective flotation to table concentration or amalgamation (on mercury tables), or to any combination of the three processes.

The mill also processed ore brought in from mines other than those on the Argo contract. It was estimated that the total production of all mines tributary to the Argo Tunnel was more than $100,000,000.[122] Major mines (mostly in Gilpin County) that provided ore to the Argo included the Gem, Sun and Moon, Frontenac-Aduddell, Saratoga, Old Town, Calhoun, and Mammoth. The California, 18,362 feet from the portal, put through $8,000,000 worth of gold, accessible from a shaft that extended 400 feet below the tunnel level. The Poso, the Prize, and the Gunnell lie far to the north under Nevadaville.[123] At the end of the tunnel at 21,990 feet, was the Concrete.[124]

In 1928, the Clear Creek County Metal Mining Association listed radium as an important product of the mines feeding the Argo, along with gold, silver, copper, lead, and zinc.[125] Because of the lead and zinc production, the tunnel remained open and active through the early years of World War II.

But on Saturday, January 19, 1943, the tunnel blew out. The ultimate end of the tunnel came when drillers penetrated old water-filled stopes of the Kansas-Burroughs mine near the end of the line on Quartz Hill in Gilpin County. The rush of water through the tunnel caused the deaths of four miners — Claude Alberts, Charles Bennetts, Sam Mathress, and Louis Hamilton — and extensive damage to the mines.[126]

As Bill Bennetts, brother of Charles, walked out to the Argo's main line to run a loaded ore train pulled by the big trolley motor to the mill, the drillers fired the shot using dangerous ten-minute fuses instead of safer thirty-minute fuses. The drillers were to use the battery-motored tram to catch up with Bennetts, who had almost made it out to the portal, lacking two or three hundred yards, when the power went off. When the rumble of the train stopped, Bill heard a terrific roar. Guessing what had happened, he raced on foot to the portal. By the time he reached open air, he was waist deep in water.

He and the outside compressor man sounded the alarm to the fire department, who blew the whistle and summoned help. It was about 4 p.m. and water totally filled the tunnel. It gushed across the portal yard, down and across Clear Creek and onto Colorado Boulevard. The water roared over the edge of the dump along the creek side, causing a tonnage of dump material to go down into the creek, creating a dam and a lake of mine waters that filled the valley. The water "boiled out" of the tunnel for many hours.

George Collins was the owner of the Kansas, one of the mines in his California Hidden Treasure Company.[127] He had boarded the bus at Idaho Springs to return to Denver and was just below town when he noticed that the creek was swollen with reddish yellow water. Stopping the bus, he got a ride back to the mill, where he nearly collapsed in shock over the accident.

Rescue efforts finally commenced at 11:00 that night, as men looked for bodies covered with mud and gravel. One was washed back toward Central City in the main tunnel.[128] The tunnel never fully reopened and the mill closed soon after.

Although the Argo Tunnel accident was a major disaster, it was not the worst one in the area. The greatest number of miners killed in one accident was in August 1895, when fourteen men drowned in the American Mine at Central City.[129]

In the 1970s, the tunnel blew out again. Apparently, huge rainstorms had caused water to collect behind a cave-in until the pile of rubble could no longer handle the load. Orange-colored fluid gushed out of the tunnel as far as what is currently the Subway sandwich shop, the bank, the post office, and the hardware store.[130]

A dream went awry in the 1990s when a local developer proposed opening the tunnel for a high-speed train to take gamblers from Idaho Springs to Central City. According to a local miner, because of the damage within the tunnel, the plan could not have worked. There were immense cave-ins and the water had bent mine rails into masses of twisted steel.[131]

The twenty-first century promises new technological advances, tested at the Colorado School of Mines Edgar Experimental Mine and the ultra modern Henderson Mine. Better extraction and processing methods may permit Idaho Springs to once again be a booming mining center.

CHAPTER SIX

A Mountain Resort

THE SARATOGA OF THE ROCKIES

I n today's hurry-scurry world, a visit to Idaho Springs is a step back in time. Many buildings and local sites are listed on the National Historic Register. The only "rush" now in Idaho Springs is the passing of thousands of vehicles speeding seventy miles per hour on I-70 through this world-class heritage site.

The hot springs set the pace in the mountain town. They seem to warm the valley, affectionately called by locals the "Mountain Banana Belt," providing grass-covered terraces where big game come to eat and drink. There were other springs along Clear Creek Valley, but those at Soda Creek stood the test of development.

In October of 1860, two miners named Howe and Miner, working along Soda Creek, came upon a headless human skeleton buried in a drift twenty-two feet down, surrounded by tree roots.[132] Further eastward, supposedly in the same bed, they found the fossil tusk of an elephant and molar teeth of a mastodon. E.L. Berthoud surmised that the human met his demise while battling with the mammoth,[133] a fact only recently accepted by archaeologists at other kill sites. Jesse Randall, writing in the *Georgetown Courier*, told the legend of a group of Mexican miners who had been working in the springs area previous to 1859. A band of Indians came upon them and killed some while others escaped "over the range" where they buried their golden treasure. Perhaps the skeleton was one of the Mexican miners.[134] Neither the treasure nor the fossils have ever been found.

When George Jackson arrived, the valley was full of mountain sheep and elk grazed on the hilltops. Mountain lions took advantage of the multitude of easy prey.[135]

Two miners, James Jack and his son, in 1860, unearthed the springs when they were digging a prospect hole through the gravel of Soda Creek to bedrock. At a depth of eighteen inches, hot water flooded their shaft. Occasionally used by citizens and travelers for bathing, it wasn't until Dr. E.E. Cummings purchased the spring property in 1863 that the springs turned into a commercial endeavor. Cummings erected a crude bathhouse and charged people to bathe in the warm, healing waters.[136] Travelers such as Bayard Taylor in 1866, weary of the dust and dirt of their stagecoach trip, visited the spring pools to rest, soak, and clean up. He wrote:

> *The soda springs are already turned to service. Two bath-houses have been built for summer guests. In one of these the water is so regulated, that the bather may choose whatever temperature he prefers, the hot spring being about ninety-five degrees as it issues from the earth. It has a deli-*

ciously refreshing and exhilarating quality, as I found after taking it warm. The taste resembles a weak and rather flat citrate of magnesia; but, as the water has not yet been analyzed, I cannot give the ingredients. The hot and cold springs come up so close together, that one may dip a hand in either at the same time.[137]

In 1908, Josiah Spurr, George Garrey, and Sydney Ball, geologists from the USGS, described three groups of springs, the Hot Springs (close together at the present Indian Springs Resort), the Blue Ribbon Springs, (cold water located just east of the present water-wheel site), and the Cold "Sulphur" Springs (several hundred yards northeast from the main spring near the historical society visitors' center).[138] The temperature of the springs ranged from 98° to 108°F or more.[139] The hot springs emerge along the contact of an intrusive body of alkali syenite with Precambrian gneiss. The Blue Ribbon Springs water came from an old adit called the Santa Fe Mine,[140] along the contact of a smaller body of syenite. It was eventually bottled, sold, and shipped all over the world as drinking water. The Cold "Sulphur" Springs rose from alluvium on the bottom of Clear Creek Valley.

Over the years, many enterprises have captured and peddled the healing heat and chemicals of the springs. The combined facilities rivaled the best in the East at Saratoga, New York. The old hotel at the Indian Springs Resort dates from 1866 when Harrison Montague, a teacher and mercantile owner, purchased the springs from Cummings. He had Dr. I.G. Pohle run analyses on the water and used that in his advertising for his "Ocean Bath:" "The medical characteristics of this spring are antacid, alterative and in many cases slightly laxative. Its external use as a bath will be found beneficial in cases of rheumatism and diseases of the skin."[141]

Richard Pearce, an eminent metallurgist and developer of the Swansea Smelter near Empire, visited the springs regularly. He isolated what he called "radium" crystals from the mineralized water and expounded on their miraculous healing abilities until his death in England in May 1927, at ninety years of age.[142] This led to the use of the name "Radium Hot Springs" for many years. The names "Vapor Caves" and "Big Soda Pool" were used at some time, at least on billboards, until the romantic Indian legends of the mountains and the name "Indian Springs Resort" supplanted the implied dangerous effects of radiation.

Montague built a swimming bath 24 x 40 feet, four-feet deep, with separate baths for ladies and men. Then the Mammoth Bath Company put up a larger building nearby with a pool 45 x 65 feet, five-feet deep. Thomas Bryan followed suit with another bathhouse in 1881 that met its demise after being converted to apartments and then to a skating rink.[143]

In the late 1800s, Dr. J.B. Finucane replaced the Ocean Wave and Mammoth Pools with a beautiful natatorium and hotel at present day

Interior of Natatorium, 1899, Teitzel photo (Courtesy Historical Society of Idaho Springs)

The Trocadero Dance Hall, 1890s (Courtesy Historical Society of Idaho Springs)

Interstate 70 and Soda Creek Road. For fifty cents, swimmers could swim in an enclosed pool 40 x 80 feet, four- to seven-feet deep, with water temperatures between 80° and 90°. An original "Water World," the pool sported a toboggan run and a trapeze.

Fred G. Shaffer built another attraction up Soda Creek, the "Trocadero." The roller-skating and dance pavilion was originally open-air, but it was enclosed when the musicians complained of having to play with gloves. A dance teacher came twice a week from Denver to give lessons in the latest dancing fads.[144]

When the Big Five Company, headed by N.C. Merrill, bought out Montague in 1890, the company enlarged the original hotel and added an elevator to take visitors to the basement. At one time, the company built a casino across the road from the hotel and numerous little resort cabins appropriately named for Indian maidens along Soda Creek. A disastrous fire almost destroyed the hotel in December 1950, but the wings were saved and the center lobby reconstructed.

The present enclosed pool was built in the 1950s and the motel across the road even more recently. The gazebo in the pool courtyard was the original gazebo built around one of the springs during the late 1800s. Today's visitors find nothing beats a dip in the hot tubs or pools of the springs after a day of skiing or a rough day on the trail.

The gazebo at the Springs — clear, clean water, early 1900s. The gazebo is now indoors on the pool deck at the Indian Springs Resort. (Courtesy Historical Society of Idaho Springs)

HEADING INTO THE MOUNTAINS

The mountains dominate the scenery around Idaho Springs. Within a short drive, the snow-capped peaks above the valley beckon visitors into the crisp, cool air. In the early days, the railroads encouraged and advertised the many splendors of the mountains.

A ride on the narrow gauge through Clear Creek Canyon was a true world-class Colorado adventure. Immense rock formations imaginatively named the "Roadmaster," under the "Hanging Rock," and below the watchful eye of "Mother Grundy," the curvy ride challenged the tenacity of even the most intrepid travelers. The first water tower stood at Beaver Brook, where a dance pavilion entertained visitors on the weekends. Next came the ghost site of a placer-village water stop called Roscoe, where visitors today often try their hand at panning gold. At the busy intersection in past days called "The Forks of Clear Creek" where the railroad splits to go either to Central City or to Idaho Springs. The hot springs of Idaho Springs usually won out over the mines and mills of Black Hawk and Central City.

In 1880, visitors to Idaho Springs could rent a double team and carriage for $10 and a room at one of the larger hotels for "$4 per day, with lower figures for permanent rates. Accommodations were, of course, first-class, with good hunting and fishing in all directions."[145] Following along Chicago

The busy depot at Idaho Springs, 1895, Lachlan McLean photo. Signs for "Big Soda Pool" and "Vapor Caves" are in distance on the left. (Courtesy Denver Public Library Western History Collection #X-2331)

Mother Grundy above the Colorado Central, 9/24/1899, Teitzel photo (Courtesy Historical Society of Idaho Springs)

Creek, the tourists rode to Chicago Lakes for an awe-inspiring glimpse of the great cirques behind Mount Rosalie, now called Mt. Evans for first territorial governor John Evans. Some hiked through the forest to the waterfalls at Devil's Canyon. Others picnicked at St. Mary's Lake at the head of Fall River. Many came to hunt and fish. In later times, owners tested their Stanley Steamers on mountain roads.

During the first decade of the twentieth century, local people picked up their shovels and went to work and created a good road up Chicago Creek,

Summit Lake from Mt. Evans, 2002, Don Allan photo (Courtesy Historical Society of Idaho Springs)

following the toll-road bed originally created by Henry M. Teller in the late 1860s. The state finished the road in 1916, aided by financing from the Federal Aid Road Act. In 1927, E.H. Honnen received the contract to complete the last mile of forest highway between Idaho Springs and Echo Lake, which made possible an alternative route to Denver via the scenic Squaw Pass Road. During the Depression, Civilian Construction Corps workers improved the road to Echo Lake, a Denver Mountain Park. Then a road was pushed to Summit Lake, and, finally, the highest paved road in the world to the top of Mt. Evans was completed. Such tourist attractions are commonplace in eastern Clear Creek County. Many adventures around Idaho Springs await visitors every day.

CHAPTER SEVEN

A Mountain Community

TOWN TREASURES

Bayard Taylor's "straggling village of log-huts"[146] has grown into a fair-sized, long and narrow town which is proud of the solid buildings built along Miner Street during the 1870s with bricks made of sediment from the Grass Valley Bar. Stately mansions built by wealthy mill superintendents and mine owners line Colorado Boulevard. Monuments and remnants of mining and railroading equipment remind visitors of this region's historical wealth.

The citizens, many of them descendents of gold miners, cling tightly to their heritage, yet live full lives in the modern day of computers and cell phones. Many, having been drawn away from the area for education or employment, return here to retain their mountain roots. A stop at the Historical Society of Idaho Springs Visitors' Center and the Underhill Museum demonstrates the pride these people have in their past.

THE CHARLIE TAYLER WATER WHEEL

The most conspicuous and curious landmark of Idaho Springs is the Charlie Tayler Water Wheel, along the south side of Interstate 70. Huge water wheels such as this one powered the mill and mine machinery. Constructed on a whim by miner Charles Tayler along Ute Creek about five miles south of town, this peculiar overshot wheel was designed to supply power for a five-stamp mill on Ute Creek. Seeing that it was doomed to destruction after Tayler's death, the executors of his estate donated it to the town in 1946. Chamber of Commerce members moved it to its present location. It is a reminder of the importance of water in the history of the valley.[147]

Waterfall and Charlie Tayler Water Wheel, 1960s (Courtesy Historical Society of Idaho Springs)

Old Smoke and Cinders, 1940 (Courtesy Historical Society of Idaho Springs)

C & S LOCOMOTIVE #60 AND CAR #70

Colorado & Southern Locomotive #60 sits across the highway from the water wheel, behind the City Hall. This old steam engine, built in 1886, rests on the rails where the railroad company left it for the city in 1941. Local railroad and history buffs maintain the engine and keep passenger car #70 in pristine condition. The car was built in 1896 by the St. Charles Coach Works, and has a capacity of forty-four passengers. It has red plush upholstering and oak interior finish. The Historical Society of Idaho Springs plans to refurbish the car's interior, including renovating the seats that were reupholstered for a movie shot there years ago.

CITY HALL

The city hall building was originally the Grass Valley School, which was doomed to destruction with the redevelopment of the east end of town. Through the actions of local citizens, the old school was moved to its present site in 1983 and is serving renewed civic duty as City Hall.

STEVE CANYON STATUE

Many visitors think the statue that stands at the intersection of Miner Street and Colorado Boulevard is of a big, strong-armed miner. However, a closer look reveals that this is cartoon character Steve Canyon.

For those too young to remember, Steve Canyon was the primary character in a long-running cartoon series after World War II. Milton Caniff, the originator of the cartoon strip, had captured the attention of national newspaper syndicates with his "Terry and the Pirates" during the war. In 1947, Caniff turned his talents to yet another cartoon hero, Steve Canyon, ace airman. In memory of the airmen who died in World War II and of the services of the Air National Guard, the Junior Chamber of Commerce of Idaho Springs decided to promote the comic strip hero. Caniff had a larger-than-life statue of the cartoon character carved from Indiana limestone. The Indiana Limestone Company covered the cost of the statue and the USAF Reserve shipped the statue free of charge.[148]

Steve Canyon welcomes you! 2004, Simmons photo

The statue was formally unveiled on July 8, 1950, at a rebirth of the Gold Rush Days. Governor Ed Johnson dedicated the work to the men who gave their last ounce of devotion in World War II and who stand ready to give that devotion again. Milton Caniff attended the ceremony, at which time the townspeople gave him two mines up Virginia Canyon along "Steve Canyon," the new name patriotic locals dubbed Squirrel Gulch in 1947.[149]

Because of the comic strip's effectiveness in selling War Bonds, one of the brass plaques at the statue's feet states, "The United States Treasury salutes Steve Canyon and through him, all American cartoon characters who serve the Nation." It is one of few statues of cartoon characters outside of Disneyland.[150] Steve Canyon often takes on other personas — dressed for Christmas as Santa or as a hard-hat miner during Gold Rush Days.

THE CASTLE

The Castle is a large stone mansion tucked away north of Colorado Boulevard. In 1881, hiring Chinese laborers, Thomas Bryan, big-spending mayor of Idaho Springs, built this immense palatial home of local granite to please his daughter. Although the home was to resemble the original Bryan Castle in England, the Chinese masons added a unique trim over the windows guaranteed to ward off evil spirits.[151]

Bryan was involved with the Bryan Tunnel in Gilpin County, the King Solomon Mines, the Inter-Ocean and Carpenter, the Colorado Tunnel, the Idaho Tunnel on Seaton Mountain, and the Hoosac Tunnel near the mouth

Tom Bryan's Castle, 1880s (Courtesy Historical Society of Idaho Springs)

of Fall River. Thwarted in his plans for an elaborate springs resort by Montague, Bryan returned with his wife to Chicago.

His son, Charles Page Bryan, represented his interests in Gilpin and Clear Creek Counties and edited the *Colorado Mining Gazette* in 1883 and 1884. Eventually, Charles served as ambassador to China and many other countries.[152]

The Castle became a hotel, then the private residence of Rees C. Vidler. In addition to his involvement with the Vidler Tunnel in Clear Creek County, Vidler and his associates built the incline railroad to the top of Lookout Mountain in Golden and worked hard to develop the parks of Denver and surrounding areas.[153]

IDAHO SPRINGS LIBRARY

The Carnegie Library sits at 14th Avenue and Miner Street. As in other communities, Andrew Carnegie donated $10,000 to fund construction of a town library. Mrs. Henry Plummer donated the land. Books from the lending library of the First Presbyterian Church filled the new shelves of the building, completed in 1904. Local ladies published a newspaper and used the profits to buy the books. For over thirty years Margaret M. Robbins was the town librarian, keeping a watchful eye on the collection of wonderful old books and maps. The library eventually preserved their old newspapers on microfilm and now provides computers with Internet access — indispensable aides to historical and genealogical researchers.

The Idaho Springs library, 1904 (Courtesy Historical Society of Idaho Springs)

One of Idaho Springs' greatest treasures, a painting of Naylor Lake by early Clear Creek artist Fred Huet, hangs in the library. Huet was an artist employed by *Nelson's Weekly* in Boston at the time of the gold rush. The paper sent him to Colorado Territory to draw the activities and scenery in the new region. Huet got hooked on gold and spent the rest of his days around Empire and Georgetown. If he needed money he would do a painting and then raffle it off at the saloons in Georgetown. Lafayette Hanchett purchased this particular beautiful painting of one of the more picturesque spots in the Rockies and eventually Helen Hanchett Williams and her husband Russell Ventress Williams donated the painting to the library in memory of her parents, Nellie G. (a library trustee at the time of the building of the library) and Lafayette Hanchett.[154]

An old arrastra was rescued from Clear Creek near Dumont and now sits in the library courtyard.[155] The cannon in the courtyard is a Civil War cannon that the local chapter of the Grand Army of the Republic obtained and placed there in 1910. For many years, the basement of the building housed the city hall and the town jail.[156]

THE SENIOR CITIZENS' CENTER

East of the library is the Queen or old Schiller Hotel. It was sometimes called the Hotel de Paris, not to be confused with the Hotel de Paris in Georgetown. In another old photo, the building bears the sign for the

The Schiller Hotel, Hotel de Paris, the Portland, or the Queen, now the Project Support Senior Citizens Center, 1880s, H.H. Buckwalter Photo (Courtesy Dan Abbott Collection, Historical Society of Idaho Springs)

Portland Hotel. The original structure, built in 1876 on this site close to the depot, was a popular hotel in town. The wooden building burned in August of 1880 and a new brick building reopened as the Hotel de Paris in October. The name "Queen" originated during the 1920s when the "King Hotel" was just up the street.[157] In 1986, the building was refurbished through the actions of local citizens into the Idaho Springs Senior Citizens' Center.[158] The best thrift store in the county fills the basement.

FIRE DEPARTMENT BUILDINGS
Directly west of the library is the old Central Hose Company (Idaho Springs Hook and Ladder Company No. 1) building, constructed in 1878 after a fire burned the local brewery and a boardinghouse. This building and the other hose company buildings around town are on the Historical Register. Antique firefighting equipment is housed in the Visitors' Center and Heritage Museum on the east end of town.

SCHOOLS
Idaho Springs' schools have always occupied the land north and west of the fire department. Originally a single-room wooden building built in 1868-69 on the corner of 12th and Colorado Boulevard served the town. An

Central Fire Hall and ore teams from the Two Bros. Tunnel, 1899, Teitzel Photo (Courtesy Historical Society of Idaho Springs)

Idaho Springs Firemen, Spider team, practicing pulling the hose cart on 7/5/1899. Teitzel Photo. See the cart on display at the Idaho Springs Heritage Center. (Courtesy Historical Society of Idaho Springs)

The old wooden school, 1885 (Courtesy Dr. Tom Noel and Denver Public Library Western History Collection #X-2370)

Idaho Springs big brick school, after 1906 (Courtesy Historical Society of Idaho Springs)

addition was added in 1880, when the enrollment soared to one hundred.[159] This structure, perhaps the oldest school structure still standing in Colorado, has been used as a home since 1885.[160]

In 1884, the townspeople contracted for the construction of a huge two-story brick school. In 1906, a trade school called the Henry Plummer Manual Training Building was added east of the main school. The Plummer family donated the money for the building.[161]

At that time, two elementary schools were built, one on each end of town. The Grass Valley School is now the city hall. The West End School is now the Baptist Church.

In 1955-56, the old brick schools were demolished and the present elementary school was built on the site. Eventually the schools were merged into today's elementary building that bears the name of two favorite sister schoolteachers, Dorothy and Margaret Carlson.

Today's Clear Creek County Middle School was built in 1969 as a high school and sits on the site of the old Waltham Mill south of Clear Creek. High school students now attend the Clear Creek County High School which was built in 2002 on Floyd Hill.[162]

CHAPTER EIGHT

Local "Ghost" Sites

THE LOST TREASURES

There was a time when residents of Idaho Springs questioned their existence, seeing their hometown listed among the "ghost towns" of Colorado. The town never has been dead. Like all communities, Idaho Springs has been a "happening place." While appearing to be sleeping, she was producing top scholars, engineers, authors, miners, pilots, and a myriad of other talented citizens. The interstate highway helped relieve the traffic jam that existed even during the '60s, when vehicles slowed to a crawl as travelers wound their way through town.[163]

Nowadays, on Sundays or after holidays, when traffic can be backed up westward for miles, travelers know to stop in Idaho Springs for a Beau Jo's Mountain Pizza Pie or a buffalo burger at the Buffalo Restaurant and Bar, with Skipper's ice cream cones or Java Mountain's exotic coffees as a treat.

Many places that existed when Bayard Taylor visited or were Lafayette Hanchett's childhood stomping grounds are now gone. Most of the mines had villages or towns nearby where the miners lived. Fortunately, through the excellent photographic record of Colorado, most of these locations have been preserved and many are being resurrected as new home sites.

LAMARTINE

Seven miles up Trail Creek Road from Idaho Springs, or at the top of a rugged 4-wheel drive called Ute Creek Road, are the remains of the high mountain town (10,610 feet) called Lamartine. The early prospectors named the mine after the poet laureate of France, Alfonse Lamartine, and the name stuck through the years.

Facing the dramatic view of Chicago Creek and Mount Evans, the village of Lamartine acted as a bedroom community for the miners who worked in the Lamartine and other mines on Alps Mountain for about twenty years. A school there served the children. The town's population, over 100 strong, drew their water from a fresh-water spring. The homes and structures were log cabins set on hand-dug terraces alongside a hillside in an open mountain meadow. The foundations of the cabins were laid of large stones on the uphill side and then filled in (or dug out) to provide a flat spot for the building. The cabins, some rather large and two-storied, were primitive compared to the clapboard buildings of the ghost town of Freeland, the nearest community and post office. However, because it was on the line between Georgetown and the Lamartine Mine, the town of Lamartine was one of the first communities in the county to have telephone and electric service.

View southeast from Lamartine showing forest-fire devastation, 7/26/1899.
Teitzel photo (Courtesy Historical Society of Idaho Springs)

The view from what few windows the cabins had was spectacular, over the neighbor's roof to the top of Mount Evans. Winter weather in this mountaintop cluster of cabins must have been severe. A local surveyor believes he has found an underground tunnel that the miners used to access the mines' workings, rather than face the storms while climbing uphill to the top of the mineshafts.[164]

The last resident of the village, a watchman for the Lamartine, died while using dynamite to blast wood out of the ground during winter in the 1920s. In the following spring, his body was found with a rock in his head from the blast.[165] Two graves are marked under the big cottonwood tree in the middle of the meadow, so Lamartine has its ghosts.

FREELAND

The town of Freeland, about four miles up Trail Creek Road from Idaho Springs, was much larger than Lamartine. Living conditions bordered on being civilized. Freeland had a post office, a school, saloons, boardinghouses, a butcher shop, a Presbyterian Church, fraternal lodge, stores, and a dance hall equipped with a brass band![166] In addition to the Freeland, many neighboring mines and mills employed the men. The lack of trees around the mines probably resulted from the logging of the forest for twenty-four cords of wood a day which was used as fuel for the Bullion Smelter, ore roasting heaps at the Freeland Mill and mine timbers, and for cabins, home fuel, and furniture.

As long as the mines were working, there were residents in Freeland. Vestiges of the more than 200 homes remain scattered throughout the forest and woodlands that have grown up since the residents left. Probably the oldest relic is the stone foundation of Captain Anshutz's mill, which was called "old" in 1879.[167] This ghost town, complete with a baby's grave alongside the road, is seeing new life as permanent residents build new houses farther up the mountain byway, now a county road.

FALL RIVER

Now buried under Interstate 70, the little hamlet of Fall River was an important way stop in Clear Creek County's early days. A toll bridge crossed the river on the road owned by Willard Teller. Bayard Taylor recalled stopping there to pay the toll man and later meeting an artist friend who was set up in an upstairs window in the hotel at Fall River, painting the beautiful scene up Clear Creek Valley. In its heyday, Fall River had two huge stamp mills, a cluster of houses and, of course, stops for stage and railroad passengers. The hamlet fell into decay when the mills closed early in the century. All that remains today is the big green sign for the intersection with Interstate 70 and Fall River Road, a mine adit, and some stone mill foundations.

ALICE AREA

The ghost town sites of Alice, Ninety-Four, and Silver City are at the end of Fall River Road. Many permanent residents now line the Fall River or the upland valleys that feed into Fall River, occupying the former ghost towns. One old hydro-powerhouse has been transformed into a quaint bed-and-breakfast, the Brookside Inn.

Alice, a stage stop on the road over Yankee Hill to Central City, was beautifully situated in a basin surrounded by stately pines at an altitude of about 10,000 feet, with several glacial mountain lakes nearby. Dependent upon the mines of the upper Fall River and Lincoln Districts (now combined into Alice), the miners and their families lived and worked at this high elevation The town was large enough to have a school, which was used by local Girl Scouts for a camp in the 1950s[168] and thus preserved.

Nearby is St. Mary's Lake and "St. Mary's Glacier," which once had the dubious but inaccurate distinction of being the southernmost glacier in North America. A healthy hike from the trailhead parking lot, the snow-field, usually present even during summer months, has never shown signs of movement — a requirement to be a glacier. True glaciers also exist much farther south in the Sangre de Cristo and San Juan Mountains. Silver Lake is a glacial "tarn lake," a lake high in a mountain bowl or cirque where a glacier once began. St. Mary's Lake could rightfully be called a "pater noster lake," a lake that fills a low spot in a glacial valley.

The village of Ninety-Four, named for the year of its settlement, lies high on Yankee Hill. It was a stage stop on the toll road from Central to Fall River. Three graves mark its site, making it a true ghost town.[169]

Silver City was one of the earliest mining camps in the Fall River District, composed of hundreds of men living in tents and brush huts housing.[170] The silver "rush" didn't last and the miners left for gold fields elsewhere.

Cabins, old and new, abound in this vacation haven as many of these ghost sites rise from the ashes. A good building site has always been a precious commodity in Clear Creek County. The city and county planners face a future full of compromise between miners, historians, and residents new to mountain life.

THE REAL GHOST TOWN

No historian would leave Idaho Springs without visiting the real ghost town, the Idaho Springs Cemetery, located high along the banks of Chicago Creek. The cemetery is at its third site. The first was situated in the block between Sixth and Seventh Avenues and Virginia Street and Colorado Boulevard. Then the cemetery was moved to the gravel terraces of lower Chicago Creek. But the site proved to be too low and high water flooded the graves. So the citizens relocated the cemetery higher on the valley terraces. Since 1874, this site has provided a dry, well-drained spot where townspeople and area residents have been buried.

In the cemetery, various organizations — the Masons, the Eastern Star, the Elks, and the Woodmen of the World — all have their sections. Large center stones with smaller stones for

Shadrach Gale monument, Idaho Springs Cemetery, 2004, Simmons photo

individual graves mark some family plots. Many marble stones show the ravages of weather and some have been knocked off their bases and destroyed by vandals.

But there's no ghost, coffin, or body beneath the gravestone of Shadrach Gale! In 1912, Gale, a Clear Creek County miner who hailed from Cornwall, took a trip home to visit his ailing parents. He booked his return passage to America on a brand new "unsinkable" ship called the Titanic. When they heard about Gale's demise upon the sinking of the ship, his fellow miners honored him with a typical Cornish wake that lasted several days. His fraternal group, the Woodmen of the World, erected an impressive red granite tombstone in his honor.[171]

The Historical Society of Idaho Springs publishes a walking tour booklet that includes the cemetery and the gravesites. It and other valuable references are available for purchase at the Visitors' Center at 2060 Miner Street, just west of the statue of Steve Canyon, the town tennis courts, and across the street from the Courtney-Ryley Cooper Park, which borders Clear Creek.

The written word cannot capture the essence of a place the way a personal visit does. The speedy drive along I-70 misses the wonders, charm, and nostalgia of historic Idaho Springs. Holding on to their deep roots like mighty oaks, the townspeople relish sharing their past experiences and history with visitors.

The champion storyteller in town is Alvin (Al) Mosch, who, along with his family, owns the Phoenix Gold Mine along Trail Creek Road. Mosch has written two books, *The Legend of the Silver Senator* and *The Hot Rock Derelicts and The Hundred Dollar Bill*, which relate his unique mining experiences in Clear Creek County during the last half of the twentieth century. Mosch and his wife, Patricia, to whom this book is dedicated, make history come alive. With their constant encouragement, people attain goals otherwise which they would deem impossible. Other residents — Marjorie and Bruce Bell, Bob Jones, Jan and Bob Bowland, Don and Carla Allan, and Dan Abbott — can recite stories, complete with dates, places, buildings, and people like talking encyclopedias. Greg Markel keeps history alive on the local radio station with monthly oral interviews of local citizens. The assistant county surveyor provided the map for this book. It is because these Idaho Springs residents shared their wealth of history that this book is possible. Local artist Caroline Jensen dug into her portfolio and provided the pen and ink sketch on the front cover.

Follow-up reading includes Lafayette Hanchett's memoirs titled *The Old Sheriff and Other True Tales*, published in 1932. *The History of Clear Creek County: Tailings, Tracks, and Tommyknockers*, the newly reprinted tome from the Historical Society of Idaho Springs, covers all of Clear Creek County and includes first person biographies of families. Other historical society publications include walking-tour booklets and newspapers, plus a wonderful first-person vignette, *Historical Highlights of Idaho Springs: Mining Camp Days* by Merle Sowell. The historical society's Underhill Museum and archives at the visitors' center contain many photographs and historical mementos.

The Idaho Springs and Georgetown Libraries and the marvelous Clear Creek County Archives in Georgetown hold county records that include early mining district and other records. Countless priceless volumes in those repositories contain Ethel Gillette's book *Idaho Springs: Saratoga of the Rockies, A History of Idaho Springs, Colorado* written in 1978, and Muriel Wolle's *Stampede to Timberline* written in 1949. Old newspapers have been preserved on microfilm. In the early 1950s, Joseph Emerson Smith wrote a series of weekly historical articles for the *Clear Creek County Mining Journal* full of juicy tidbits that he gleaned during years of editing the *Denver Post*. *The History of Clear Creek and Boulder Counties* and Frank Fossett's *Guide to Mines and Ranching in Colorado*, both published in 1880, are invaluable resources. The standard source of early mining information is James Ovando Hollister's *Mines of Colorado*, written in 1867 by the editor of the Central City newspaper, *The Register*. Government publications include exhaustive reports from the United States Geological Survey — *The Economic Geology of the Georgetown Quadrangle*, Professional Paper 63 by Josiah E. Spurr, George H. Garrey, and Sydney H. Ball in 1908, and Edson S. Bastin and James M. Hill's Professional Paper 94 on the *Economic Geology of the Central City District and Idaho Springs*. Smaller bulletins from the Geological Survey by J. E. Harrison and J.D. Wells describe the conditions of the region's mines and their locations after World War II during the uranium boom.

On a broader scale, the Colorado Historical Society and the Denver Public Library post the most extensive western history photograph collection on the Internet, some of which they contributed to this work. They, and most of the other local libraries or historical societies, have complete genealogical research sections, some of which are online.

A great helper on this project was Kathy Honda, interlibrary loan technician at Auraria Campus Library in downtown Denver. She constantly spotted and turned up important papers, articles, and references that had probably not seen the light of day since publication. Kathy Thomas of the *Rocky Mountain News* and Dr. William Wilson, a resident of Georgetown, historical researcher, author, hydrologist, and weather watcher, also rendered editorial help.

Colorado is a treasure chest of history where nuggets of information lay deeply buried. Pan and prospect to find the strike of a lifetime! This book is the first lesson in learning about Colorado history as told by those who find Idaho Springs a delightful place to visit, study or reside. Enjoy your sojourn!

Endnotes

1 Wallihan, S. S., 1871, *The Rocky Mountain Directory and Colorado Gazetteer*, Denver, Colorado, Wallihan, Compiler and Publisher, p. 369.

2 Note on the back of a photograph of George Andrew Jackson taken in Ouray, Colorado, at the Denver Public Library states, "I was fifty-five years old on the 24th of last month. August 20, 1889." This makes Jackson's birth date on July 24, 1834, so in 1858, he would have been 24 years old.

3 Rickard, Thomas A., 1897, "The Development of Colorado's Mining Industry," *Transactions of American Institute of Mining and Metallurgical Engineers*, V. 26, p. 334.

4 Wilson, William E., Winter 2003, "Louis Vasquez," Colorado Heritage, Colorado Historical Society, p. 3-15; Wilson, William, 4/10/2004, personal communication.

5 Rickard, "The Development of Colorado's Mining Industry," p. 334.

6 Whitney, Joel Parker, 1906, *Reminiscences of a Sportsman*, New York, Forest and Stream Publishing Co., p. 138.

7 Jackson, George A., 1859, in Spring, Agnes Wright, 1959, April, "Rush to the Rockies, Centennial Edition," *Colorado Magazine*, V. 36, #2, pp. 82-129.

8 Ibid.

9 Ibid.

10 Ibid.

11 Ibid.

12 Ibid.

13 Ibid.

14 Ibid.

15 Ibid.

16 Byers, William, April 23, 1859, *Rocky Mountain News*, p. 2, col. 2.

17 Spring, "Rush to the Rockies, Centennial Edition," pp. 82-129.

18 Ibid.

19 Ibid.

20 Ibid.

21 Smiley, Jerome C., 1901, *History of Denver*, Denver, Colorado, Denver Times Publishing, p. 286.

22 Mosch, Patricia, 3/17/2004, personal communication.

23 Smith, Duane A. and Moriarty, John, 2002, *The Ballad of Baby Doe: I Shall Walk Beside My Love*, Niwot, CO, University of Colorado Press, p. 29.

24 Burke, John, 1989, *The Legend of Baby Doe: The Life and Times of the Silver Queen of the West*, Lincoln, NB, University of Nebraska Press, p. 19.

25 Ibid, p. 35.

26 Ibid, p. 71.

27 Ibid, p. 116.

28 Ibid., p. 238, note 13.

29 *Rocky Mountain News*, 8/29/1863, p. 2, c. 1.

30 Ibid.

31 Hollister, James Ovando, 1867, *The Mines of Colorado*, Springfield, MA, Samuel Bowles and Co., p.234.

32 Wallihan, S.S., 1871, *The Rocky Mountain Directory and Colorado Gazetteer*, Denver, Colorado, S.S. Wallihan & Company, p. 127.

33 Jones, Bob, 3/17/2004, personal communication; Bowland, Jan, 3/17/2004, personal communication.

34 Miller, Richard A., 1969, *Fortune Built by Gun, The Joel Parker Whitney Story*, Walnut Grove, California, Mansion Publishing Co., pp. 31-33.

35 Whitney, J.P. 1867, *Colorado, Schedule of Ores, Paris Exposition*, London, Cassell, Petter, and Galpin, p. 22.

36 Old, R.O., 1869, *Colorado, United States, America: Its History, Geography, and Mining Including a Comprehensive Catalogue of Nearly Six hundred Samples of Ore*, London, England, British and Colorado Mining Bureau, p. 72.

37 Smith, Joseph Emerson, 1951-1954, "History column," Idaho Springs, Colorado, *Clear Creek County Mining Journal* weekly issues.

38 Smith, Duane, 2002, *Henry M. Teller, Colorado's Grand Old Man*, Niwot, CO, University of Colorado Press, p. 21.

39 *Rocky Mountain News*, 1884.

40 Frost, Aaron, 1880, "Idaho Springs, Its mines and mineral water," Georgetown, Colorado, *Georgetown Courier;* Whitney, Joel Parker, July 1867, "Letter to Central City residents," Central City, Colorado, *Central City Register.*

41 Digerness, D.S., 1982, *The Mineral Belt, Georgetown, Mining, Colorado Central Railroad*, V. 3, Silverton, Colorado, Sundance Press, p. 271.

42 Ibid, p. 274.

43 Ibid, p. 271.

44 Ibid, p. 274.

45 Historical Society of Idaho Springs, 1986, *History of Clear Creek County, Tailings, Tracks, & Tommyknockers*, Denver, Colorado, Specialty Publishing, p. 74.

46 Dempsey, Stan, 11/17/2002, personal communication.

47 Frost, Aaron, 1880, in Baskin, Orin L, ed., 1880, *History of Clear Creek and Boulder Valleys, Colorado*, Chicago, Illinois, O.L. Baskin, p. 331.

48 Laws of the Union Mining District, Clear Creek County, October 21, 1861, Resolution 1 as quoted in Whitney, J.P., 1865, *Silver Mining Regions of Colorado with some account of the different processes now being introduced for working the gold ores of the territory*, New York, D. Van Nostrand, p.88.

49 Mining Laws of the Russell District, Gilpin County, Sect. 67 as quoted in Whitney, J.P., 1865, *Silver Mining regions of Colorado with some account of the different processes now being introduced for working the gold ores of the territory*, New York, D. Van Nostrand, p. 97.

50 Mosch, Al, 11/15/2002, personal communication.

51 Dempsey, Stan, 11/17/2002, personal communication.

52 Gillette, Ethel Morrow, 1978, *Idaho Springs: Saratoga of the Rockies*, New York, Vantage Press, p. 154.

53 Fossett, Frank, 1880, *Colorado: its Gold and Silver Mines, Farms and Stock Ranges, and Health and Pleasure Resorts: Plus a Tourist's Guide to the Rocky Mountains:* 2nd Edition, New York, C. G. Crawford, Printer and Stationer; Sowell, Merle, 1976, *Historical Highlights of Idaho Springs, Mining Camp Days,* Historical Society of Idaho Springs.

54 Gillette, *Idaho Springs,* p. 137.

55 Frost, in Baskin, *History of Clear Creek and Boulder Valleys, Colorado,* p. 332.

56 Fossett, *Colorado: its Gold and Silver Mines,* pp. 372, 373.

57 Spencer, Elma Dill Russell, 1966, *Green Russell and Gold,* Austin, Texas, University of Texas Press, p. 158.

58 *Rocky Mountain News,* 8/29/1863, p. 2, c.2.

59 Harrison, Louise, 1974, *Empire and the Berthoud Pass,* Caxton, Idaho, Big Mountain Press, p. 111.

60 Ibid, p. 112.

61 Ibid.

62 Ibid, p. 70.

63 Mosch, Al, 3/12/2004, personal communication; Harrison, J.E. and Wells, J.D., 1956, *Geology and Ore Deposits of the Freeland-Lamartine District, Clear Creek County, Colorado,* USGS Bulletin 1032-B, Plate 8.

64 Hollister, *The Mines of Colorado,* p. 239.

65 Harrison, *Empire and the Berthoud Pass,* p. 42.

66 Jackson, in Spring, "Rush to the Rockies, Centennial Edition," p. 82-129.

67 Bastin, Edson S. and Hill, James M., 1917, *Economic Geology of Gilpin County and Adjacent Parts of Clear Creek and Boulder Counties, Colorado:* USGS Prof. Paper 94, p. 158.

68 Hollister, *The Mines of Colorado,* p. 239.

69 Ibid., p. 240.

70 Ibid.

71 Ibid., p. 241.

72 Ibid.

73 Ibid.

74 Ibid.

75 Wolle, Muriel Sibell, 1949, *Stampede to Timberline: The Ghost Towns and Mining Camps of Colorado,* Denver, Colorado, Sage Press, p. 108.

76 Spurr, Josiah, Garrey, George H., and Ball, Sydney H., 1908, *Economic Geology of the Georgetown Quadrangle, together with the Empire District:* USGS Prof. Paper 63, p. 814.

77 Eberhart, Perry, 1969, *Guide to the Colorado Ghost Towns and Mining Camps,* Denver, Colorado, Sage Press, p. 62.

78 Bancroft, Caroline, 1990, *Unique Ghost Towns and Mountain Spots,* Boulder, Colorado, Johnson Books, p. 16.

79 Ibid., p. 15.

80 Eberhart, *Guide to the Colorado Ghost Towns,* p. 62; Brown, *Jeep Trails to Colorado Ghost Towns,* p. 27.

81 Michaels, David, 1974, "Black Eagle Mill; The nuts and bolts of it," *Clear Creek Almanac,* p. 20.

82 Ibid., p. 22.

83 Mosch, Al, 11/29/2002, personal communication.

84 Ibid.

85 Bell, Marjorie, 2/14/2002, personal communication; Vigil, James, 2/11/2002, personal communication.

86 Historical Society of Idaho Springs, data list.

87 Spude, Robert L., 2003, "The Ingenious Community; Georgetown, Colorado, and the Evolution of Western American Silver Milling and Metallurgy, 1864-1896," *Mining History Journal*, Vol. 10, p. 113.

88 Meyerriecks, Will, 2002, *Drills and Mills*, Tampa, FL, self-published, p. 212.

89 Gillette, *Idaho Springs*, p. 64.

90 Meyerriecks, *Drills and Mills*, p. 195.

91 *Colorado Miner*, 6/10/1882, p. 2., c.2.

92 Hollister, *The Mines of Colorado*, p. 238.

93 Ibid., p. 152.

94 *Argo Tailings*, 1998, p. 1 (Souvenir newspaper from Argo Mill).

95 Ibid.

96 Historical Society of Idaho Springs, *History of Clear Creek County*, p. 74.

97 Spude, "The Ingenious Community; Georgetown, Colorado," pp. 124, 125.

98 Rickard, "The Development of Colorado's Mining Industry," p. 397.

99 Bastin and Hill, *Economic Geology of Gilpin County, Colorado*, p. 158.

100 Meyerriecks, *Drills and Mills*, p. 91.

101 Ibid.

102 Mosch, Al, 11/25/2002, personal communication.

103 Gillette, *Idaho Springs*, p. 198.

104 Meyerriecks, *Drills and Mills*, p. 82.

105 Mosch, Al, 11/25/2002, personal communication.

106 Rickard, "The Development of Colorado's Mining Industry," p. 334.

107 Gillette, *Idaho Springs*, p. 167.

108 Historical Society of Idaho Springs, *Tailings, Tracks, and Tommyknockers*, p. 49.

109 Bell, Bruce, 3/23/2004, personal communication.

110 Gillette *Idaho Springs*, p. 75.

111 Hanchett, Lafayette, 1932, *The Old Sheriff and Other True Stories*, New York, Margent Press as quoted by Gillette, *Idaho Springs*, p. 76.

112 Halloran, J.A., *Mining and Scientific Press*, 1896, March 14, p. 211.

113 Gillette, *Idaho Springs*, p. 85.

114 Halloran, J.A., *Mining and Scientific Press*, 1896, May 9, p. 383.

115 Aldrich, John K, 1997, *Ghosts of Clear Creek County*, Lakewood, Colorado, Centennial Graphics, p. 37.

116 Gillette, *Idaho Springs*, p. 83.

117 Aldrich, *Ghosts of Clear Creek County*, p. 37.

118 Stewart, K.C. and Severson, R.C, 1994, *Guidebook on the Geology, History, and Surface-Water Contamination and Remediation in the Area from Denver to Idaho Springs*, CO: USGS Circular 1097, p. 25.

119 Sowell, *Historical Highlights*, p. 62.

120 Bastin and Hill, *Economic Geology of Gilpin County, Colorado*, p. 158.

121 Aldrich, *Ghosts of Clear Creek County*, p. 37.
122 Clear Creek County Metal Mining Association, 1928, p. 12.
123 Ibid.
124 Sowell, *Historical Highlights*, p. 58.
125 Clear Creek County Metal Mining Association, 1928, p. 11.
126 *Argo Tailings*, p. 1.
127 *Argo Tailings*, p. 3.
128 Sowell, *Historical Highlights*, pp. 66-67.
129 *Georgetown Courier*, 1895 August, as cited in the "Annals of Clear Creek County," 9/29/1944, weekly column, Georgetown, Colorado, *Georgetown Courier*, Issue #19.
130 Mosch, Al, 3/13/2002, personal communication; Kittredge, John, 3/12/2002, personal communication.
131 Mosch, Patricia, 3/18/2004, personal communication.
132 *Western Mountaineer*, Oct. 25, 1860.
133 Frost, in Baskin, *History of Clear Creek and Boulder Valleys, Colorado*, pp. 273, 362.
134 Mosch, Pat, 1985, "Who were the first Clear Creek Miners?," *Front Range Journal*.
135 Jackson, in Spring, "Rush to the Rockies, Centennial Edition," p. 82-129.
136 Wallihan, S. S., p. 369; Clear Creek County Records, Book C, p. 491, James and William Jack transfer to E.S. Cummings lots and claims along Soda Creek; In 1865, Cummings preempted the rights to the mineral waters.
137 Taylor, Bayard, 1866, *Colorado: A Summer Trip*, ed. Savage, William W., Jr., and Lazalier, James H., 1989, Boulder, Colorado, University of Colorado Press, p. 73.
138 Spurr, Garrey, & Ball, *Economic Geology of the Georgetown Quadrangle*, p. 164.
139 Ibid.
140 Gillette, *Idaho Springs*, p. 159.
141 Ibid., p. 144.
142 Ibid., p. 159.
143 Ibid., p. 154.
144 Ibid., p. 158.
145 Fossett, 1880, *Colorado: its Gold and Silver Mines*, p. 96.
146 Taylor, *Colorado: A Summer Trip*, p. 72.
147 Gillette, *Idaho Springs*, p. 206.
148 Young, Roz, 7/19/1997, "Milton Caniff: Steve Canyon Turns 50 this year, No Monument Here; Colorado has One," *Dayton Newspaper*, p. 15A.
149 Flanagan, Mike, 4/24/1983, "Out West," *Denver Post Magazine*.
150 http://www.roadsideamerica.com/map/co.html.
151 Historical Society of Idaho Springs, *Tailings, Tracks and Tommyknockers*, p. 349.
152 Gillette, *Idaho Springs*, p. 154.
153 Gillette, *Idaho Springs*, p. 156.
154 Hanchett, *The Old Sheriff and Other True Stories*, p. 59; Plaque on the painting in Idaho Springs Library.
155 Historical Society of Idaho Springs, *Walking Tour*, July 4, 2001, p. 1.
156 Gillette, *Idaho Springs*, p. 167.

157 Bell, Marjorie, 3/17/2004, personal communication.
158 Historical Society of Idaho Springs, *Walking Tour*, July 4, 2001, p. 2.
159 Historical Society of Idaho Springs, *Tailings, Tracks and Tommyknockers*, p. 135.
160 Bell, Marjorie, 3/23/2004, personal communication.
161 Historical Society of Idaho Springs, *Tailings, Tracks and Tommyknockers*, p. 135.
162 Bowland, Jan, 3/17/2004, personal communication.
163 Gillette, *Idaho Springs*, p. 189.
164 Markel, Greg, 10/12/2002, personal communication.
165 Mosch, Al, 2/16/2001, personal communication.
166 *Colorado Miner*, April 8, 1882, p. 3, c. 7; June 3, 1882, p. 3, c. 8.
167 *Colorado Miner*, March 29, 1879, p. 2, c. 3.
168 Bowland, Jan, 3/17/2004, Personal communication.
169 Aldrich, *Ghosts of Clear Creek County*, p. 28.
170 Aldrich, *Ghosts of Clear Creek County*, p. 29.
171 Historical Society of Idaho Springs, *Walking Tour*, p. 54.

Index

CPSIA information can be obtained at www.ICGtesting.com
Printed in the USA
BVOW022349080212

282471BV00007B/16/P